D0714000

FEMININE SENSUALITY

Alcira Mariam Alizade

FEMININE SENSUALITY

Alcira Mariam Alizade

translated by
Christine Trollope

Foreword by
R. Horacio Etchegoyen

London
KARNAC BOOKS

First published in 1999 by
H. Karnac (Books) Ltd.
58 Gloucester Road
London SW7 4QY

Spanish edition: *La sensualidad femenina,* © 1992, Alcira Mariam Alizade; published by Amorrotu Editores, Buenos Aires, Argentina

British Library Cataloguing in Publication Data

A C.I.P. for this book is available from the British Library

ISBN 1 85575 097 X

10 9 8 7 6 5 4 3 2 1

Edited, designed, and produced by Communication Crafts

Printed in Great Britain by Polestar Wheatons Ltd, Exeter

To my sons, Ariel and Juan Martin—to life . . .

CONTENTS

PREFACE ix

FOREWORD by *R. Horacio Etchegoyen* xi

Introduction 1

1 The sense of the body 9

2 The body in psychoanalysis: the nucleus of stone 25

3 Feminine orgasms 61

4 Feminine virginities 113

5 The dissolution [*Untergang*] of the Oedipus complex in women 127

6 Faithfulness–unfaithfulness 139

7 On passion and passionate sensuality 151

8 Feminine masochism: eroticism and the human condition 163

REFERENCES AND BIBLIOGRAPHY 171

INDEX 179

PREFACE

Writing this book has been an adventure, a journey across an ocean of words—a journey undertaken in passion, where my ship was in constant danger of foundering on hidden reefs.

I want to thank so many friends who supported my task. The names flood in, and I have often merely scratched in their initials to record my gratitude.

I am delighted to present these pages in which I intend to sort out from my practice some variables that play a role in female sensuality, whose origins lie in both the body's animality and in its vast spirituality.

Contributions from Freud onwards are many. It was impossible to go through them all before publishing this essay. Time was short, and much valuable material had to be omitted.

I also thank the authors who helped me in my work of thinking, whether their bias was in the direction of admiration or opposition. In both cases they gave me the opportunity of fruitful confrontations that contributed to the progress of my book.

Special thanks to Didier Anzieu for having looked at parts of this text and wishing me courage in my venture as an author.

FOREWORD

R. Horacio Etchegoyen

Female sexuality has always been in the forefront of psychoanalytic research. Freud was at first inclined to believe that the characteristics of boys' infantile sexuality were also applicable *mutatis mutandis* to girls, but was later compelled to recognize that the matter was not so simple. At any rate, from the time of the *Three Essays* and even earlier, Freud always maintained that the organ of infantile genital sexuality was the penis and that both sexes discovered the vagina only at puberty. So it was that he built up his theory of sexual monism (or phallocentric theory), which became ever more consolidated and coherent as the years passed. A decisive point on this journey was reached with Freud's tardy realization—as he himself said—that, just as there were an oral and an anal stage in libidinal development, so too there was an infantile genital organization that was phallic, in that both boys and girls recognized only the penis as an organ that might be present or absent, whereas the vagina did not exist.

Many prominent psychoanalysts, and a man who knew psychoanalysis and women very well, rebelled against the monistic theory of sexuality and demanded that women be accorded an equal position with men—and one that was, moreover, different from theirs—while at the same time asserting that girls knew and recognized the vagina. (Although this is a basic empirical fact, it is always amenable to theoretical discussion.)

There was a moment in history when it was possible to locate these two opposing conceptions of female sexuality geographically, the first in Vienna—on the continent of Europe—and the second in London—in the British Isles. In his famous paper for the Wiesbaden Congress of 1932, "The Phallic Phase", Ernest Jones (1933) declared himself to be *plus royaliste que le roi* in categorically rejecting Freud's assertion made a year earlier that it was "*only in the male child that we find the fateful combination of love for the one parent and simultaneous hatred for the other as a rival*" (Freud, 1931b).

This polemic continued unabated and then, as we know, spread throughout the world after the tragic *Anschluss* of 1938. With the subsequent progress of research, the dualistic theory of sexuality gained more and more adherents, as witness the publication in 1964 of *Female Sexuality*, edited by Janine Chasseguet-Smirgel (English edition, 1970), in which a group of eminent French analysts decisively espoused Jones's position. At the same time—or more precisely a few years later—a revisionist trend arose among the American ego-psychologists and culminated in the appearance in 1977 of *Female Psychology*, edited by Harold Blum.

* * *

The fact that Alcira Mariam Alizade's book is called *Feminine Sensuality* is not due merely to a concern for semantic precision; still less is the title a play on words, because her fundamental thesis, to my mind, is that women must study, understand, and conquer themselves through their sensuality, for all that anatomy may be their destiny.

The author clearly states her views in the most important chapter, "Feminine orgasms": "*I am aware that my position has a controversial tinge and that it is at variance with orthodox conceptions of how women approach pleasure and sexual enjoyment.*" The plural is used because the forms and locations of the female orgasm are more varied than those of its male equivalent and because it is not necessarily a single entity, as it is in men. On the other hand, given the human race's innate bisexuality, the female orgasm may also be encountered in men, even if women have easier access to it.

The concept underlying Alizade's argument is surely Didier Anzieu's skin-ego, and her guide throughout is the baby's experience of satisfaction at the breast as the model of orgastic satisfaction.

The skin-ego is the precursor of the ego proper; anchored in the epidermal integument, it contains the image of the self, where tactile sensations, whether endogenous or exogenous, and active and passive alike, allow the subject to distinguish between *inside* and *outside*, thereby supplying the foundation for the organization of the ego of the affects and drives. Yet the ego is not merely an outer integument, for we must also postulate the existence of a psychic locus of pure stone that affords protection from narcissistic wounds and sustains self-esteem.

In the *Three Essays* Freud had described the effects of a breastfeed as a kind of orgasm, which would constitute the model for all sexual satisfaction in adult life. That was the basis of Radó's explanation of melancholia in terms of the feeding orgasm, and it is also the starting point of our present author, who considers that this *primordial orgasm*—as she calls it—is the predecessor of all the individual's future erogenic experiences. The primordial orgasm expands to cover the entire surface of the body and precedes the difference between the sexes and the notion of conflict, at a time when the self-preservative and the sexual drives operate in unison. As the backcloth to our erotic lives, the primordial orgasm is a prelinguistic experience in the service of primary narcissism and of the pleasure principle; it is ultimately "*a primary form of pleasure involving the death drive fused with the life drive*".

While the primordial orgasm is the matrix of all adult sexuality, by virtue of its qualities it is understandably more readily applicable to women than to men. It provides a foundation for comprehending the different forms in which the various erotisms will combine to make up women's rich libidinal potential, whereby the orgasm can flourish in the most disparate circumstances. It is interesting to note that in Alizade's view men do not understand female sensuality, partly because of the difficulty they have in accepting women's erogenic overflowing. From this standpoint the persistent attempt to accommodate the female of the species in the procrustean bed of the male orgasm is a way of constraining, dominating, and controlling her. The author concludes that fantasies of female erogenic overflowing not uncommonly lie at the root of sexual pathology in both men and women.

* * *

All in all, then, this is a passionately written and passion-arousing volume that not only brings the male reader close to the Eternal Feminine—to the dark continent so dreaded by Freud—but also gives women more trust in their feminine condition. This translation offers the English-speaking psychoanalyst a chance to see these problems in a new light.

I therefore sincerely commend the book to all.

Buenos Aires

FEMININE SENSUALITY

INTRODUCTION

This book is in a certain way a history of the events of intimacy, a chronicle of the erogenous events that occur in a woman's body. Today, at the close of the twentieth century, the night-gown that apparently covered our great-grandmothers' bodies, with a single opening near the genitals to make sexual intercourse possible, has been removed, and women have begun to say something, as soon as it could be said, about the sensual changes repressed by civilization and prohibited by sectarian orders—"the fruit of the will to domestication carried out by the authorities" (Firpo et al., 1984, p. 11).

I intend to bring out, if only partially, the vicissitudes of the meetings, struggles, and delights between bodies, or those of a body with itself, in psychoanalysis with the aim of contributing to the unravelling of the skein of questions by which femininity has been invaded. A question with no answer—what does the woman want?—is symptomatic of an attitude that ascribes to the woman a certain marginality concerning knowledge of the wants of her body, and finally of herself.

The taboos are weakening thanks to the fields women have conquered and the human urge for truth, which goes beyond the mercenary struggles and narcissistic pathologies by which we are invaded.

Woman is emerging equipped with a language that has shed all devaluation and embarrassment. Her speaking body is beginning to give a glimpse of the light in the "dark continent" (Freud 1926e, p. 212), which is becoming illuminated without ceasing to cling to the secret, intransmittable, obscure aspects that constitute the yearning depths of every human subject. Behind the idea of feminine sensuality, difficult as it is to understand, there is hidden an erogenicity that is different in that it largely escapes biological laws and brings into play erogenous emotional shades that are disconcerting both for men and for women themselves.

The body, that strange and powerful ruler of our destiny, surrounds itself with capital letters, just as a material in which we are clothed moulds itself to our outline. At the same time, it confronts us with the subversion of the flesh—that is to say, with its revolutionary shock in a paradoxical dimension that is simultaneously close to biology and far from it. There are tremors that arise in the depths of the soma, from the first anchor-points of the erogenous body, interwoven with sensations and perceptions that advance from the roots of corporeality to reach the most complex strata of the human soul.

The body, almost denuded of itself, drops its disguises and reveals, through living flesh, an ineffable enigma, and paths are plotted on its material aspect that do not follow an ordered linearity, nor a prolix and unmodifiable development.

These pages will look alternately at the flesh—a perceptible living substance—and at the soul, which embodies the notion of a sense in itself and introduces the ethics of the body, a controversial subject. We shall pass from unleashed sensuality in an interchange of desire in which pleasure and enjoyment play a part to the description of a fleshless sense, in its own container, protected from instinctual demands—an area of domesticated pleasure that includes a covering of malleable and firm skin-ego (D. Anzieu, 1985), a body in itself and for others only after that, a mediatized body. To the five senses (sight, hearing, touch, taste, smell) I add this invisible sense, which implies the elevation of the senses above corporeality and the approach to a nucleus-point of pure stone, where there is room for the transcendental, the beautiful, and the sublime. Sensuality needs this feeling to become finally separate from all that is animal and perverse.

Thus a line forms, in successive steps, of the biological body, the body of sense-perception, the erogenous body, the emotional body, the body through which language passes, the ethical body, and the social body influenced by the demands and models of the cultural environment.

I prefer to speak of feminine "sensuality" rather than "sexuality" because my quest is for the sensorial matrices and the experiences that register the first viscero-sensitive–erogenous characters that will acquire a new meaning later. Sensuality may be compared to freely floating energy, which, if it is more easily expressed in the erogenous zones of the orifices (mouth, anus, vagina), which are privileged areas for the enjoyment of pleasure, also expands over the whole surface of the body, without respect to the area of the skin or to any bodily orifice. In addition, sensuality appeals to the senses whose stimulation can give rise to an enormous voluptuousness that is totally alien to the physiology of sexuality.

The erogenous body resembles a Moebius strip in which the external and the internal follow each other without discontinuity; it moves from surface to depths, from skin to viscera.

Erogenicity takes its place as a property that can impregnate a part of the body such as a sense or a function, either to inhibit or to facilitate it. Sexual significance, in suddenly involving an act that is apparently anodyne, gives it "erogenicity" (Freud, 1926d [1925], p. 89). Starting with this conception of erogenicity, female sensuality unfolds along new lines, and a woman's erotic life may be considered from a different point of view. As we shall see later, this affects, to a large extent, the way we shall face the great theme of female orgasms and question the presumed frigidity of women.

I want to introduce another area respecting feminine sensuality: that of fluidification and secretion. The emissions involved in it are those secreted by a body moved by excitation and emotion. This fluid world can easily be made to seem dirty and dishonest, that which bodes ill, a world of impurities that ooze from the skin and from the orifices of the body. It is interesting to note in this respect that during many epochs in the course of history a crust of dirt on the body represented a mark of honour (Perrot, 1984, p. 27), the grimy body saying through its dirt that it had not been touched even by water, that its filth was an attribute of the immaculate. This is a body wrapped in a cloak of dirty purity—that of the young girl who thus confesses her lack of sin by showing off a body that is not demanding to be pleasured. The vesture of dirt hides the possible scandal of living flesh, open and disposed to gaining erotic pleasure from its own or another body.

The feminine element is far from bringing into the present the image of the repression and passivity of the women in Freud's consulting-room in 1900. Mythology and ancient history are full of references in which the woman appears as greatly valued, endowed with active power, a warrior goddess, vengeful and quick to anger. Desroches-Noblecourt (1986, p. 20), in his book on women in the time of the Pharaohs, points out that the notions of femininity and of justice are closely linked with cosmic equilibrium in almost all religious legends and myths. For example, the Egyptian myth of the eye of the god Ra is highly illustrative. It is a feminine, wandering eye, which escapes from the god and flees through the world. When Ra, tired of waiting, replaces it, the anger of the eye is so intense that in order to placate it Ra has to place it on his forehead. The eye is later transformed into the symbol of power and protection in the form of a female cobra. It is also called "the distant one" and can change into a raging lioness, spitting fire from her eyes.

The feminine element lifts up its powerful voice, which can be heard in culture. When we take up the theme of the witch, we shall consider again the multifaceted aspects of the feminine.

I am also conscious that by approaching the field of "the feminine" and by considering women, I am introducing a certain artificiality in that I am excluding "the masculine", as though the two elements were not closely interwoven in every human subject, from constitutional bisexuality onwards. Nevertheless, from all possible levels of approach, the feminine element does apply to the woman to a greater degree, as the masculine element does to the man. This does not, however, alter the certainty of Leclaire's (1979) reflection about how difficult it is to give an adequate definition of sex from a psychoanalytic point of view.

What makes feminine sensuality so attractive is its very complexity. Perception, sensation, emotion, affect, erogenicity, ties with an object, circumscribe this sensuality. It is this body in its feminine aspect—a mass of experiences as the subject "is"—that is the goal of my considerations. I claim a lordly place for the emotional body (chapter three).

I also want to mention in this introduction the pseudo-liberation of bodies in which, beneath the appearance of "all being permitted", the erogenous interchange imitates the gymnastics of pleasure, which is almost compulsory in the service of the repression of emotions.

Nevertheless—and I leave the question open—do we not perhaps need a little of these gymnastics of pleasure for good psychic functioning, to frighten away the shadow of the actual neurosis and to shut the doors to anxiety? Is civilization not excessively attached to rigid clichés and ego-ideals, which now block the erogenous outlets and now over-facilitate them, advocating promiscuous circulation of bodies without any emotional commitment? How can one circulate among bodies, obtaining pleasure while at the same time respecting the erogenous object and oneself? There arise in my mind the images evoked by Margaret Mead about sexual liberty in the Island of Samoa (quoted by Langer, 1951, p. 48), where the only taboo is that of incest and where couplings seem to take place without conflict, by pure instinctual need, pure physiology, which is joyfully satisfied while the life of the natives flows on.

Immersed in civilization, human existence comes up against obstacles. Psychoanalysis has taken it upon itself to bring to light certain complexities regarding erotic object-life.

Is there not often an unconscious object, a wife or mother, lurking behind a manifest object-relation with a man? And vice versa?

Is not an amorous encounter sometimes provoked or wrecked in a second by a sudden phantasy? Does not the play of identification perhaps show its subtle influence in object choice and in the difficulties that bedevil human love-relationships? Does the *senti* (what Spitz called the coenaesthesic universe: D. Anzieu, 1970) that comes into play in interchanges with other significant elements not perhaps allude to an endless sequence of resonances in the interweaving of representations, emotions, and sensual perceptions? In the exercise of sexuality, do not sometimes the life instincts, sometimes the instincts of destruction, predominate?

In this book I am talking about a body that is simultaneously sensitive and experiencing perpetual interactions between the affect and the representation, between the primary process with its various strata of unconsciousness and the organizations that impose the secondary process, a body at the mercy of conflicts, of passions, of the snares of pleasure and the tricks of identification, of object-illusions in the service of the satisfaction of narcissistic and oedipal phantasies. The language and the deep emotions provoked by the beings that circulate upon human flesh leave tracks, marks, trophic wrappings or lacerations, roughnesses and caresses upon it.

Beginning first with the body of pure pleasure, the body-mass demanding gratification allied with the ego of pleasure, I deal in turn with the gradual transformations of that body as it spies out other regions in which it can become detached, due to its condition of being subject to the language of its own flesh, on the road to sublimation and spirituality, while at the same time—the human paradox—it is submerged in regressive movements, to the extent of its possibilities, towards what is primitive, original, archaic.

In the presentation of female sensuality, I have included a chapter on the first meetings and partings, the "matrices" of psychism that affect the quality of the sense-experiences of life. [In various chapters of this book I have been supported and inspired by the valuable contributions of Didier Anzieu in his concept of a skin-ego (1974, 1985) as a primary basic phantasmatic cover for the somato-psychic integrity of the individual.]

I proceed from there to the inner elements of femininity, the area of virginity rooted in sensuality, and the revirginizations linked with the capacity to wait. The active passivity of the woman accompanies us like the figure of the "cirularity" that Lou Andreas-Salome (1899) confers on woman in her destiny as carrier and supporter of wrappings and in her privileged role of "giving" in maternity and in her sublimated substitutions.

It is not difficult to observe, from the anatomical and physiological substratum, how life and death are embodied in a woman's body. She appears as supporting the mystery of life and death in that she engenders life by giving birth to children and shows her closer link with death in the vulnerability of her body to blood (menstruation, childbirth, abortion). The enigma is on her side—above all, the enigma of the unconscious, which she embodies (Assoun, 1983, p. 11).

And, unfortunately, human beings do not have good relations with death. Either they seek it, fascinated, destroying themselves and destroying their fellow beings, or they deny it and try to escape it by imagining themselves to be immortal. As I understand it, if there has been so much talk of feminine sexuality as enigmatic sexuality, it is not because it is so enigmatic or because masculine sexuality has no secrets, but because the feminine element lends itself to the embodiment of the great enigma of creation. This is what Gauguin expressed so beautifully in his marvellous painting, "Whence do we come? Who are we? Where are we going?"—a threefold question, a handful of unknown quantities for a humanity dismayed by the fact of existence. This coincides with the first question asked, according to Freud (1908c, p. 212), by every child: "Where do babies come from?" Freud points out how the idea of the universality of the penis makes it impossible to reply to this question. Thus he clearly shows the way a baby will attribute a penis to the woman at the very moment when he intuitively feels the presence of something the inside of which is a receptacle and also produces babies. The orifice, the tunnel of the vagina, that royal road to the fertilizing interior of a woman, becomes intolerably obvious. Once again, anatomy is destiny, in this case generating anxiogenic phantasies. Then the woman, too, will have a penis. It is better not to think of the inside of a woman's body; it is too exciting and disturbing.

The idea that "everybody has a penis" takes its place as a certainty that obstructs the psychic openness to new plans of action on the one hand, while at the same time bringing relief, since from the splitting of sex without a penis there emerges something sinister, something that must be known and is impossible to know. It is the incarnation of the lack of being that constitutes the human person.

The feminine element seems to epitomize a truth the power of which is different from that exerted by civilization, fighting to defend various narcissistic achievements.

Finally, "feminine" is not a synonym for "woman". A woman attains femininity through psychosexual movements that make her consubstantial with her feminine being. She will then be a feminine woman. The feminine in men and the play between various attitudes in the same woman are also due to bisexuality.

The enigmatic nature of feminine sexuality, which has so often been emphasized by psychoanalysis, must not make it impossible for us to strip away the "x", the unknown quantities, even when this unveiling (like all unveilings) appears in an asymptotic form.

At some points I go beyond the limits of the title and face more abstract problems on the fringes of the human condition, such as female masochism, the function of "taking on a body", fidelity and infidelity, or the difficult approach to the nothingness that lurks in civilization like something impossible to represent. In those last chapters, feminine sensuality becomes blurred, and there emerges the human subject who vacillates from one position to another (masculine and feminine).

Even so, in this book psychoanalysis keeps very close to the body—a body that feels, vibrates, and is repressed, a body that depends on its fellow beings, is caught up in its conflicting instincts, and is inhabited by gods and demons.

CHAPTER ONE

The sense of the body

In this chapter I consider as a whole those experiences that play a part as phenomena in the sense of the body and attempt to show the complexity of erogenous experience in its intimate interaction with sensoriality. "Experiential mass" is the name that I give to the body that is in a state to receive stimuli while at the same time reacting to these stimuli in ways that are unique to each individual. All individuals have their own fund of sensitivity, the different components of which are mingled in a particular formula, and this again will vary according to circumstances and to the dominant psychopathological structure.

Some general principles

1. Fundamentally, there are two planes that influence the instinctual world—the sensorial and the representational.

2. The sensorial plane can be divided into three strata: the perceptual, that of the sensations, and the affective.

3. Erogenous experience circulates between experiences, emotions, perceptions, affects, and representations. Two considerations arise at this point:

a. There is individual variation with respect to the amount of libido and sexual requirements. Freud said that "it is one of the obvious social injustices that the standard of civilisation should demand from everyone the same conduct of sexual life—conduct which can be followed without any difficulty by some people, thanks to their organisation, but which imposes the heaviest psychical sacrifices on others" (1908d, p. 192). To listen to erotic demands from the psychoanalytical point of view implies shedding prejudices and ideologies and accepting a wide variety of needs and inhibitions that range far beyond convention. Vicissitudes in object-relations, the dimension of human love, conflicts of loyalty—all these divert the course of the erogenous impulses and allow for successful sublimations and forms of erotic relationships that challenge the physiology of sexuality, bringing substitute satisfactions, and ego-orgasms (Winnicott, 1958) that offer profound well-being in the context of indirect instinctual satisfactions.

b. The importance of the concept of instinct is disputed, as Didier Anzieu points out in the epistemological preliminaries to his book, *The Skin-Ego* (1985). Nor is the list of instincts closed. Freud himself divided them three times, first distinguishing between instincts of self-preservation and sexual instincts, then between ego-libido and object-libido, and finally between the death instincts and the life instincts. But in addition to these classifications he left isolated passages in which he gave other names to instincts. Thus in his work on jokes (1905c) he conceptualizes the "urge to communicate the joke" (p. 143), on the basis of a term coined by Moll: the "instinct of contrectation" [*Kontrektationstrieb*]—a type of social instinct that impels us each to make contact, one with the other. In this text Freud makes repeated use of the verb "to impel" (pp. 142, 154–156), referring to the force that peremptorily urges one to pass a joke on to others. He also predicates the existence of an "impulse to dominate" (1905d, 1913i, 1915c)—a non-sexual instinct whose aim is to dominate the object by force.

Later investigations produced the important contributions of Bowlby (1969) on the instinct of attachment, and those of Imre Hermann (1930) on the instinct of apprehension. They are instincts concerned with contact with the primary object. They include—as do the theories of Spitz—the idea of another person, significant as psychic food for the preservation of life. In this instinct sexual elements co-exist with those of self-preservation. They help me to reflect on the value of the function of "taking on a body" throughout life (see chapter two).

4. I firmly emphasize the huge distance that separates animals from humans. Rooted in animal corporeality, in its quality of subject of the language, and bearing a code of affects, the human being separates itself from its own biology and transforms the material elements that have gone into shaping it. Thus every general law trying to define the pleasure of the senses remains disputed.

5. The area "before the word" is fundamental in the sense of the body. It includes the field of the unutterable, the innumerable, of somatizations, of dynamics and somatic communications instinctually cathected. Words count as "things", their symbolic content is contingent. They are "missile-words", or "armour-speech", "action-language", words that hide, speech sited "beyond words" (Schust-Briat, 1991). We note the paralinguistic effect of words of pure acoustics, of pre-verbal signifiers. These signifiers were conceptualized by Rosolato (1985) and Didier Anzieu (1987). Rosolato calls them "demarcation signifiers" and compares them with representations of things. These signifiers originate in early infancy, and may precede the acquisition of language. He proposes the following list of opposed pairs for demarcation signifiers: pleasure–unpleasure, good–bad, presence–absence, inside–outside, passivity–activity, oneself–others.

Similarly, Rosolato points out the importance of the analogical gesture that allows mutual understanding to occur without words, establishing a common element based on sympathy, which argues that there exists a terrain of reciprocal identification that is somatic and tactile.

Didier Anzieu prefers to call them "formal signifiers", that constitute not so much the "objects" that form the basic unconscious psychic contents as the psychic containers. Further on he adds: "They allow impressions, sensations, and ordeals that are too early or too intense to be put into words to be committed to memory" (D. Anzieu, 1987, p. 11). They impose themselves on the psyche as ineffable.

Formal signifiers are intimately attached to the bodily scheme, and special sites in the moving body. They can be pathological or non-pathological. They all allude to phenomena that take place on an original plane of psychic function, closely linked with experiences of the bodily ego. With his investigation Didier Anzieu enters the pre-representational world, related to pictograms (Aulagnier, 1975) and to the archaic concept of hysteria (McDougall, 1986).

The phantasmal stimulation that takes place in a sensual body-to-body situation favours the revival of these formal signifiers in the climate of regression that may accompany the encounter. The amazing dimension of the destruction of form, of strange bodily changes, even touching on something sinister and nightmarish, helps us to understand the distance on contact, the limitations and controls with which many subjects go through their sensual life.

"Beyond words" and "before words" are seen as fascinating realms for psychoanalytic exploration in the world of somato-psychic adventures.

6. Sensuality works within a "determined context", which includes both the social and the cultural ambience and public opinion, with its criteria and taboos about what is considered an optimal sexual life within the established canons. The superego watches over sexual satisfactions and affects the quality of experiences. As an example, I would mention the enormous value set on homosexuality in ancient Greece, and the high esteem in which the temple prostitutes were held in certain religions—holy women, called "the divine donors of their bodies" in Tibet (Monestier, 1963).

7. The sense of the body can appear in an autoerotic form or in relation with another body. In the first case, the play is with objects of phantasy internally linked. The direction of the uncon-

scious in the sense of its tireless orientation towards pleasure governs the way to erogenous sensorial stimulation. This allows a certain control of the sensual situation and its interruption when intolerable representations or affects arise. In the second case, the vulnerability of the subject is greater, in that in the intersubjectivity with another body the interchange is subject to surprise, to a share of the unforeseen, to a different look that is narcissistic or disqualifying in effect. And, above all, once the sexual act is over, there remains an impregnation with the vibrations of the experience, a sweet or bitter taste, according to the illusions awakened, the affective use that has taken place, the approval or disapproval of the superego, the narcissistic wounds, the expectations of loving and being loved, and so on.

Notes on perception and sensation

Perception is the process through which a living organism becomes conscious of stimuli. Perception is always perception of a relationship. It constitutes what is given immediately, the first to be given. It is the function that attends, successively, to the stimuli that flow constantly and are entered in the record of sensations, affects, representations. The world is perceived from that accumulation of flowing instantaneous events. The collection of impressions links the different perceptible qualities one with another.

The living body is a mass that feels, a burning mass, continually shot through with images, sounds, pressures, odours. These perceptions are associated with imprints on the memory and then involve memory function (Freud, 1900a, "Regression"). Perception immediately decodes the various perceptions with which it is bombarded, starting with the pleasure–unpleasure polarity in a conscious or unconscious form. Recollections of perceptions enter the memory. To the sensorial perceptions derived from outside events impressed on the five senses are added perceptions derived from the interior of the body (kinaesthetic, self-perceptive, etc.). One step further, and we encounter the affective perceptions: a look of hate, a scornful laugh, a wounding word, an aggressive pressure, a breath of love. . . .

Freud (1900a) worked out a scheme linking the perceptive with the motor pole. Perceptions are conscious by definition; responses at a motor level are not. Stimuli set in motion "incipient movements" (Merleau-Ponty, 1945, p. 209), which are associated with the quality perceived, forming a sort of halo around it. The perception rapidly installs itself as a sensation that prolongs the earlier one and echoes through the responses it generates.

The sensations or perceptible qualities show their motive physiognomy "enveloped in a living significance" (Merleau-Ponty, p. 209). They consist of various attributes: quality, intensity, extent, duration. Analysing the sensorial world enriches the approach to sensuality by allowing access to "a life of my eyes, of my hands, of my ears, which are so many other natural egos" (p. 231).

The mass of experiences affords a glimpse of the fabric of which it is composed, the partialities of which it is constituted, the fragments that mark every love-life. One "is" one's body beyond what is imaginable, in that one inhabits a first corporeality marked out by affects, experiences, and the inexhaustible universe of language.

Perceptible experience is a vital process, which puts us in contact with the world about us. At the same time, the invisible is taken up in the visible when we are connected with parts of our body that we do not see or which we shall never see, which we perceive obscurely and sketch in our thoughts (Merleau-Ponty, p. 205).

Merleau-Ponty makes a profound study of perception and sensation from a phenomenological point of view. I want to highlight the richness of his observations on the interchange between the sensor and the sensible, between qualities, or, if you like, between the external sensations that irradiate a certain life-style with their "power of magic" and the sensor, the one who goes in search of them through an act of the senses. He says:

> The sentient and the sensible do not stand in relation to each other as two mutually external terms, and sensation is not an invasion of the sentient by the sensible. It is my gaze which subtends colour, and the movement of my hand which subtends the object's form, or rather, my gaze pairs off with colour, my hand with hardness and softness. . . . Apart from the probing of my eye or my hand, and before my body synchro-

> nises with it, the sensible is nothing but a vague beckoning. [p. 214]

This is a beautiful description of a meeting of two bodies that mutually perceive each other and feel each other, alternately occupying the place of sensor and sensible, in which the quality of magic impregnates the atmosphere and sensations are potentiated and displayed on the background of the natural egos of the parts of the body that attract or repel each other. The sensorial functions are redistributed in the body, reviving, so to speak, the basic vicissitudes and properties of corporeality, moving from the category of the living to that of the inanimate. Merleau-Ponty writes: "As every sensation is, strictly speaking, the first, last and only one of its kind, it is a birth and a death".

It is a profound communion of the senses, which acquires a different dimension when the body is in the situation of having had sex—that is to say in an affective context in which the attraction of the object and the capacity of receptivity towards it acquire the greatest relevance. Now the senses are covered in an erogenous wrapping and seek an object that will acquire existence by either desire or love. One plane covers another, and the sensory-perceptive stimuli begin to be under the direction of sexuality.

If, as Merleau-Ponty says, "every sensation implies a germ of a dream or depersonalisation" (p. 215), the blossoming of this germ allows us to watch the world of voluptuousness (see chapter three), in which sensations are transformed, change their qualities, are thrown into confusion, change places with each other in a movement of regression, while desire is blindly uniting one body with another.

Sensitivity varies from one moment to another. It depends on the differential thresholds in relation to the attributes of sensation. There will be bodies that are more or less sensitive, and bodies that are specifically sensitive to definite stimuli. For that reason, every sensual experience is unique, and any generalization in that field is impossible.

I want to emphasize the profound, immeasurable value of the world of the senses, the conglomeration of experiences anchored in the live productions of the sense of the body, in which the essential circulates, adhering to the flesh, the eye, rhythm, temperature, pressure, colour, the perceptible universe of sensoriality.

"The perceptible has not only a motive and vital significance, but is no more than a certain manner-of-being-of-the-world which proposes itself to us from a point in space, which our body picks up and assumes if it is capable of doing so, and sensation is, literally, a communion" (Merleau-Ponty, p. 225). It is a communion with the world without words, in a primal language, a language of the skin and the viscera, a code of archaic affects.

The space of the skin-ego

The skin-ego (D. Anzieu, 1985) is a precursor of the ego anchored in the epidermic covering that contains the image of oneself. As early as 1970 we find a precursor of the skin-ego in the concept of *senti*, which Anzieu formulates in close relationship to what Spitz called "the co-enaesthetic universe". Anzieu includes the notion of sensorial coverings, among which he mentions the "bath of words" or "bath of prosody" that the *infans* receives from its primary object. One of the principal functions of the skin-ego consists of distinguishing the outside from the inside, what belongs to me from what does not belong to me. He writes (1990):

> . . . the projection into the psychism of the surface of the body, that is to say the skin, constitutes that doubleness, that interface, to speak in modern scientific terms, which is the ego. In fact, tactile experience possesses the peculiarity in relation to all other sensorial experiences of being endogenous and exogenous at the same time, active and passive. . . . Tactile sensation allows the basic distinction between the 'within' and the 'without'. . . . I am speaking of the skin in its incidence on the psyche, that is to say what I have called the Skin-Ego.

Among the many functions of the skin-ego I should like to quote those of *holding* of the psyche, of support and container of the inner world and of sexual excitation, of localizer of the erogenous zones, and of the recognition of the difference between the sexes.

In my perusal of the sense of the body, I come across this basic imaginary structure for the linking or rule of the inaugural perceptive and instinctual disorder.

The skin-ego as precursor of the ego rooted in the biological body is a primal starting-point for thinking of the trophic flow of sensuality. It is an imaginary intermediate space, which links the archaisms of the senses, affects, and partial instincts, enveloping them in its phantasmatic covering of skin, in its own *Gestalt* [*Ichgestaltungen*] from which the subject organizes his affective and instinctual ego.

The functions of the skin-ego are eminently at the service of the life instinct. It is enough to look through the pages of Anzieu's book to prove this observation, even when Anzieu does not disregard the connections with the destruction instinct and perverse fixations or masochism.

The skin-ego is required as an intermediary between the mother and the infant in the process of fusion or individuation. To be armed with a good skin-ego implies the emergence from the inaugural chaos of early psychic experiences biologically supported in an imaginary container provided by the epidermic envelope. This means to be "decked out" with all the bio-psychological arsenal that is germinating untidily in the new being. The acquisition of a limit, a barrier between oneself and the external world, is a positive consequence. Didier Anzieu (1985) writes: "The installation of the Skin-Ego responds to the need for a narcissistic covering and assures to the psychic apparatus the certainty and constancy of basic well-being" (p. 30).

The skin is the first covering of the skin-ego. Within are multiple coverings (this notion of covering goes hand-in-hand with that of skin-ego) both sensorial and affective (of anxiety, suffering, etc.). All these coverings constitute "a pre-individual psychic cavity endowed with a sketch of unity and identity" (p. 150).

It interests me to think of the skin-ego as a black box, using the terms of the theory of communication, in which the components of the experiential mass (sense-perceptions, affects, pre-verbal and linguistic meanings) go in at one end, and at the other, brought about by this phantasmal organization, there emerge conscious and unconscious motor effects, new sensations and experiences, forms of instinctual discharges, eroticisms.

First encounters. First non-encounters

Between a human being and the expectation of having a child many phantasies are born. In the desire or otherwise for carrying a child, in the real or imaginary intention of conceiving it, a dynamic set of representations and affects comes into play, directed towards a non-existent being which regains psychic reality from that moment and begins to creep in as a virtuality. These are the psychic babies of which one dreams and which slowly take shape in the nooks and crannies of the history of human desires.

The child becomes a project conceived in the parents' hopes, an imaginary body defined by the parents' hypotheses.

Later still, the "coming one", the "foetal being", the "embryonic ego" receives echoes of these desires in the wide range of loves and hates that express them. Here are enchained the phantasies of the sex it will have and, a step beyond, the fascinating theme of its own name and its vicissitudes. The child becomes a "spoken shadow" (Aulagnier, 1975).

In the act of birth, the infant loses its psychosomatic protective coverings, though it may not be for more than a fraction of a second. It is born "in living flesh", without the protective muscular and aquatic membranes. Otto Rank speaks with good reason of the birth trauma, designating with that expression the sudden change and the influx of intense and sudden stimuli to which the newly born is subject. Annie Anzieu (1974) describes it excellently: "The chaos of the body, maddened and smooth, moist and tepid. The new emptiness of floating without liquid". It is in dreams that the subject, once adult, will find again substitutes for the foetal membranes and will recreate the lost Paradise (Garma, 1949). As soon as it is born, various wrappings—material (linen cloths, shawls) thermic, olfactory, visual, and so on—protect it from the external world. The mother's body becomes the main covering and fulfils externally the enveloping function that biology meant it to provide within. From "one body for two" it is transformed into "one skin for two". The somatic skin will have to be constructed at the psychic level in the gradual constitution of a skin-ego.

In the beginning, the same covering enwraps mother and child. The necessary cutting back of a covering for them—that is, the detaching of the primal object—constitutes a kind of second birth for the psyche looking towards exogamy. This differentiation opens the way to autonomy and individuation.

This is an example of a trophic cut.

It is important to point out that certain breaks occur of necessity (the term "crisis" can translate them clinically), so that even when they bring suffering, they allow the breaking, the tearing apart of the rigidity of a suffocating covering, and the passage towards the constitution of a sort of "web of psychic regeneration", the skin-ego becoming modified in this way in the sense of achieving greater plasticity. An intense crisis, an acute wound may occur in the "royal road" for the elaboration of phantasms, the resolution of which makes it possible for that subject, as he passes through a painful flaying, to acquire a "new" skin and have access to other psychic regions. It is the positive aspect hidden in the negative, the protective function of a "covering of suffering" (Enriquez, quoted by D. Anzieu, 1985). Tears, withdrawal, pain, anxiety, and so on involve the wound and give the subject the opportunity, supported in his covering of suffering, quietly to take the necessary time in his inner world to recompose himself. But the break is an inevitable step. On other occasions the coverings have a defensive function: they form a protective skin that enables the subject to avoid a greater evil, namely the revelation of the fissures and nakedness of a damaged skin-ego (Bick's "muscular second skin").

The pathological breaks can be categorized from the first non-encounters. We can read in them the opposite phantasy to that which Freud described in 1915: instead of "His Majesty the baby", we have here "His Enemy the baby". The baby as enemy carries the filicidal impulses (Rascovsky, 1973), Medea's dramatics (Alizade, 1988a). The infant will be dethroned from the magnificent seat of honour of narcissism, and archaic conflicts will visit the surface of its bodily ego. The breaks that it will have to suffer will intensify the negative force of the original phantasms, condemning the subject to re-live painful exclusions, traumatic castrations, and seductions.

In addition, not all are "phantastic wombs" (Cachard, 1981, p. 850), idealized magic intrauterine spaces in which apparently omnipotence and immediate satisfaction reign. There are many dismal legends of birth, internal acts of violence, conscious desires for death, "survivals" in advance. Freud wrote (1914c) that "biology is at the base of all psychological provisions". What is the place of violence in a gestating womb? How can we read the possible effects produced on the foetus? The study sends us back to works on foetal psychism (Rascovsky, 1973; Rascovsky & Rascovsky, 1977). To the physical blow is added the psychic blow when a father curses the embryo the arrival of which is announced at the wrong moment, or a mother accepts with resignation the disgrace of an unwanted pregnancy (see observation of Mary, in chapter two).

The pre-birth baggage of the human being interacts with the medium. This sort of prenatal *senti* is a primal psychic organizer.

Envelopes and breaks come one after the other. A psychic wound may, if protective coverings are not received in time, penetrate to the somatic body (it is at this point that the problem of psychosomatic protection is raised).

In the play of intersubjectivities a psychic skin may either involve another (similar) one trophically for the benefit of *Eros* or may, in the realm of *Thanatos*, tear off the other's skin and damage it where the bodily ego takes root in the speaking flesh of a desiring subject. In this latter case there predominates the pathology of a crushing intersubjectivity in which one "cries out for the skin of the other", sometimes to procure with the other's tearing the very integrity of its envelopes. We are facing the drama of narcissistic tearing apart and the negative ferocity that is evident, for example, in the clinical picture of pathological divorces.

Envelopes and breaks

The intersubjective effects that take place as a result of the encounters and non-encounters of a subject in interchange with the other significations of his surroundings may be conceptualized in the light of two imaginary forms: the envelope and the break.

These forms correspond to two psychic movements that unfold in the field of intersubjectivity, namely: (a) circularity; and (b) linearity. Circularity is involved with the concept of psychic envelope, and linearity or punctuality with that of the break or psychic cutting. In the first movement it is the category of continuity that is at play, and in the second that of discontinuity. Both can be enlisted on the side of normality or pathology. We thus have envelopes that relieve, protect, and caress, and envelopes that suffocate, distress, destroy, intoxicate.

Breaks, in their turn, can be harmful (damage, psychic wounds) or trophic, in that they constitute cuts that provide freedom from a rigid envelope or from reorganizing crises. The break in this latter case interrupts a pathological continuity.

The world of the senses, affects, and ideas sketches, in the interaction between psyches, different types of envelope and different types of break.

Observation of Teresa

In relation to the sense of the body, feminine sensuality, and the concept of psychic envelopes, Teresa's session, which I describe below, allows me to observe:

1. the associative succession of different psychic envelopes;
2. the bridges joining sensoriality to erogenousness;
3. the continuity between perceptible images of the external body and of the internal body;
4. the prime importance of sensorial stimulation and of the coming into play of impulses of an inhibited aim in feminine sensuality.

The senses are interwoven with instinctual movements. Sexuality, subordinated to sensuality, facilitates the display of profound and intense experiences. The oscillation between sensoriality and erogenousness potentiates the voluptuousness of the senses in the field of eroticism.

> As soon as she has lain down on the couch, she breaks a short silence by saying: "There's the smell of another person, a smell as if another person has been here." When I ask her what feelings the smell gives her, her reply is sharp: "I don't like it. It is the smell of a man or of a woman without a woman's smell, a

dirty woman." Immediately she complains that my armchair, placed a little more to one side than usual, lets me see her better. "Why are you to one side? So that you can see me?" she reproaches me in an annoyed tone. I point out to her my rejection of the envelopes, olfactory and visual, that are unfolding in the field of the session. The "smell of another" is close to the phantasy of the primal scene. Annoyed, she tries to break my enveloping eye contact. The following associations bring new unpleasant smells: shit, cigarettes, dirt. "Either I do not recognize the smells of places, or I am smelling very intense odours. Today I looked at my shoes, and I smelt shit." The associations recall her mother, who smokes, and the grimy intimacy of mother and daughter. She then goes on to refer to erogenous feelings. She says: "Sometimes I would like them to touch me in another way, to be gentler, not so rough. . . . I pretend to be a very hard person, not very delicate, but I am extremely sensitive to touch, and I set much store on delicacy. Nevertheless, all men are very coarse." Teresa is alluding to the missing envelope of the body of a boyfriend who broke with her abruptly. She is also expressing her sensual dissatisfaction, since she often experiences sexuality as violence, as flaying, and the pleasure obtained from sexuality is small compared with the sensual affective unpleasure that accompanies it.

Subsequently she takes up again the subject of her olfactory experiences, and she tells me that nauseous odours produce acidity in her. She has associated them with her internal body. I ask her whether she was a vomiting baby. She replies: "I do not know, but I do know that when I went in a car I felt sick and vomited for the whole journey. The vomiting is not only vomiting . . ., the acidity gives me nausea, which is almost nastier than the remedy I take." The following representation takes her back to her erogenous feelings: "It made me feel sick when I sucked X. Retching. It made me feel sick, and that will end up in my mouth." I point out to her her rejection of milk. Immediately she tells me that she takes milk only as a remedy against acidity. "I hate it by itself, everything inside is rotten."

This last phrase synthesizes Teresa's image of herself. Alone, she hates herself and finds nothing healthy to recover. But we can also hear the demand for a "good-enough" body to help her to form an entire skin-ego, a malleable bag that will make her feel "comfortable in her skin" and allow her to have a healthy image of her inner self.

Sensations, senses, erogeneity, and the body in its epidermic and orificial aspect are interwoven in this short fragment of the session.

When I point out to her that at the previous session she accepted the good milk that I gave her but that today she vomited and felt that it was a drink that disgusted her, she replies, to my surprise:

"It is also certain that when I look back on the last few years, I realize there was a time when I did not feel so good, I feel relieved, more comfortable, and for years I could not say this. . . . I feel like talking with my parents, I believe I am in another place, in a new place . . . of course, after all, I come back to being the same, as usually happens."

When I go back over this session, I reflect that what comes out after my interpretation proves that in the course of the analysis we have been putting together a common skin, which relieved her primal anxiety that she had been exposed to abandonment.

I am interested in bringing out from this vignette the intimate association between sensoriality and erogeneity. The two elements form a sort of Moebius strip such as the external body forms with the internal body. Therefore, when Teresa rejects my visual sensorial covering, she is showing her defence against a possible erogenous transference. To be looked at makes her slide from the sensorial to the sensual.

The category of the sensorial points to the world of the erogenous.

CHAPTER TWO

The body in psychoanalysis: the nucleus of stone

Quiero volver
a aquella certidumbre
al descanso central, a la matriz
de la piedra materna.
[I want to return
to that certainty
to the central repose, to the matrix
of the maternal stone.]

Pablo Neruda, *Piedras del Cielo* [Stones from Heaven]

Freud wrote (1900a): "I believe it is allowable for us to give free course to our hypotheses, provided we keep perfect impartiality of judgement and do not take our feeble shell for a building of absolute solidity. As what we need are auxiliary representations which help us to reach a first approximation to something unknown, we shall use the most practical and concrete material."

In this way, as an auxiliary representation, I have to introduce the notion of a psychic place of pure stone, bare, in the very centre of gravity of the psychic apparatus. The place of stone occupies an internal space without sex, an imperturbable matrix that procures the "central repose" (to paraphrase the poet) of stone. This centre of gravity supports the psychic apparatus. It is like that minute fragment of inorganic material that must be at the centre of the oyster so that the pearl can develop.

Noel Altamirano (1990), in his book on Neruda, mentions the symbolism of the "centre" studied by Mircea Eliade. In Eliade's opinion the centre symbolizes absolute reality, sacredness, and immortality and is characterized by being well defended. The place of stone as I postulate it has a certain connotation of the absolute and perennial; it is, rather, a nucleus of stone that needs no defence. It "is" invisible non-corporeality. Perhaps the "domestication" of the instincts depends on getting this nucleus firmly established (Freud, 1937c) and on the capacity to submit to the rule of the overflowing exuberance of the senses and to cope unscathed with "self-regard" (*Selbstgefühl*, Freud 1914c, p. 98).

The nucleus of stone has no evolutionary meaning. A first outline of this nucleus emerges when sucklings distinguish themselves from their mothers and begin to feel unique. Stern (1985), in his exhaustive study of the infant's interpersonal world, distinguishes different levels in the appearance of what he calls "sense of self" (sense of the emerging self, sense of the nuclear self, sense of the subjective self, sense of the verbal self). These concepts closely interact with the nucleus of stone. To the first manifestations of this stone place are added trophic narcissistic envelopes, constructive speculations, identifications. A psychic space is taking shape, which, though it originates in interaction with the medium, is separating from it to constitute *solitude in itself*, vitality independent of the outside world, the pure primal name of simply "being", a plane of equilibrium. This place is consolidated—or not—throughout life, constituting a point of energy, a centre of strength for the psychic apparatus.

It is a psychic place that is difficult to picture, related to ethics and to mental health. Its genesis and consolidation can be looked at from a theoretical point of view or by recourse to one's own subjectivity. It is a sort of abstraction. At the same time, inferences from clinical data make it possible for us to observe phenomenologically the presence and the effects of this seat of equilibrium. The nucleus of stone is a sarmentum that supports the subject. The somato–psychic unit functions synergically at the command of this trophic stone nucleus. In the place of stone, structural identifications have intervened, and there are experiences accumulated in the record of pain and satisfaction. On being precipitated into the inner world, the flesh disappears, and now, starting with the work of decantation, the characters of fiction fall back and the subject remains alone, without anyone and by himself. In his own solitude, constructed from many companions and experiences, there builds up alone the place of pure stone, the unharmed space on which I intend to theorize. As it incorporates itself in erotic life, the place of stone protects the subject from narcissistic hurts and underpins self-esteem. By its very nature, the place of stone is free from tearing and flaying. Of course, it is stone—eroded by time but a rock of strength—or, in the positive sense, it is living rock.

The place of stone can be detected in allusions in clinical material that semantically refer back to ideas such as skeleton—support, framework, ownership, integrity. There are hints of experiences of a central mass and of the qualities of constancy, stability, solidity. I emphasize the idea of the nucleus of stone being "unfleshed" to illustrate its lack of perceptible materiality, its non-sensuality, the absence of impulse, of movements of desire, of everything that disturbs a subject in mind and body. This place of stone is a point of connection that intervenes in the unconscious drives of the subject's life. It endows him with the feeling of ownership of himself and allows him to maintain the stability of his inner world. The nucleus of stone helps to produce the unique character of that particular subject. And it is unique in that the trophic narcissistic coverings added to this nucleus give it a feeling of self-evaluation *"per se"*, independently of the concrete goals achieved or the failures suffered. A positive "I am", without attributes, enters the subject's experience quite naturally.

The notion of stone constitutes a reference point, a space of self-arrest, of "apprehension of oneself".

In analytical practice we often observe things lacking in the make-up of this space. Analysis will seek to acquire experiences that could consolidate this nucleus. It must try to reach, within the transferential link, some of the most delicate aspects of the patient's mind, the primary misunderstandings.

The element that protects the nucleus of stone can be understood in the light of Thom's concept of catastrophe (1980). Thom first developed the catastrophe theory in mathematics. "Catastrophe" means the change from one system to another. This change can occur through the destruction of the previous system (here "catastrophe" coincides with the accepted definition—for example, an exploding boiler) or, and in this lies the revolutionary import of this theory, "catastrophe" implies a mutative change, a sudden leap by which the system escapes destruction. The flexibility and agility of the operation and a determined mathematical form intervene in both cases (closed form in the case of the destruction of the system, open form in the case of the leap from one system to another).

The nucleus of stone accompanies every point of the displacement of the open curve, promoting the leap to another system. It thus protects the system from destructive explosions, from violent breaks. Through the mutative leap from one system to another as crises—in the form of non-disastrous catastrophes, mere simple catastrophes inherent in the condition of being alive, chaotic experiences that reorganize the inner world at another level—occur, the nucleus of stone helps to avoid them. The system that is able to mutate instead of being closed is alternately closed and in a curve (Thom, 1980, p. 62)—that is, it is an open system.

The consolidation of the nucleus of stone equips the subject to display a good aggressive potential, the healthy ferocity of a trophic violence that not only deflects the death instinct but also impels the subject to penetrate the exogamous spaces. At this point the nucleus of stone is articulated, giving openings to existence, inner freedom, and the access to creativity.

Psychic envelopes and the nucleus of stone

Didier Anzieu (1985) theorized on the skin-ego, the first narcissistic envelope on which the feeling of well-being is based. Similarly, he has dealt with the pathologies of the skin-ego and has extended his investigations to the multiplicity of psychic envelopes that comprise it. The creation of envelopes is a condition of psychic functioning. Anzieu says they possess three basic functions: those of container, of interphase or limit with the outside world, and of training for the interchange of communication.

Psychic envelopes show various degrees of malleability and rigidity. They may be normal or pathological. They have movements like that of fusion (union with another skin in the phantasy "one skin for two"), tearing (see chapter one), and accumulation, one upon the other, in the form of multiple envelopes. There exist developments and metamorphoses of the envelopes (see the case of Diana, in this chapter).

It can be said that there exists "an instinct to envelop oneself". This instinctual force would tend to generate *circular movements that constitute psychism.* Instinctual dynamics come to pass in three periods, namely: (a) One is enveloped. In this first period the *senti* (D. Anzieu, 1970), constituted of various sensorial envelopes, enwrap the infant from its birth. The word of the others who matter, especially the mother, surround it with an accompanying "bath of voice" or "bath of prosody". (b) One is enveloped by oneself. It is a reflective period, an internalization of the function of being enveloped. The complementary series determines the quality of these envelopes, whether they are normal or pathological. (c) One envelops another. This instinctual movement can arise from pathology (symbiosis, envelopes of two with violent breaks in sadomasochistic links) or from normality (access to love, to caring for one's fellow beings).

It may be inferred that the instinct to enwrap oneself may be found in the service of either the life instinct or the death instinct. Thus Didier Anzieu (1985) shows how preconscious phantasies of fusion and unconscious phantasies of tearing apart co-exist in masochism.

Sometimes the envelopes act as a mask and attempt to compensate for and replace the deficit in or non-existence of a nucleus of stone. In this case the psychic envelopes (see the observation of Diana, in this chapter) show a compulsive character, which hides an intense primordial helplessness [*Hilflosigkeit*]. In the work of analysis we are present at the gradual dissolution of these compensatory auxiliary envelopes, and, as though in counterpoint with them, the nucleus of stone will gradually come to exist. This is expressed clinically through the following psychic parameters:

a. the experience of beginning to "be in oneself" or to "belong to oneself";
b. intrinsic valuation of oneself, independently of the connotation of success or failure attached to it;
c. a greater feeling of inner security;
d. the capacity to exist alone.

Observation of Diana

To clarify and illustrate these ideas, I give some fragments of Diana's analysis. The material allowed me to consider:

1. the succession of associations between different envelopes;
2. the deficit in the installation of the nucleus of stone;
3. the compensatory nature in the face of the non-existence of a central nucleus of pathological envelopes—an envelope of suffering, a toxic (hallucinogenic) envelope, and compulsive sensual bodily envelopes—that showed the compulsive order described earlier;
4. the incipient birth and later consolidation of the nucleus of stone through the analysis of two dreams;
5. the gradual dissolution of pathological envelopes.

Before going into the consideration of the first dream of this young analysand, I should like to relate a recent episode in her life, work on which at the session facilitated Diana's introspection and the later elaboration of her constitutional deficits.

Let us come to the story.

> Diana tells how, on the occasion of a festival, having drunk and smoked too much, she found herself in bed in an intense orgy of pleasure. Later she became distressed. She felt herself in love with one of the young men who were with her that night, and vehemently desired to have a child by him. He remained indifferent to her manifestations. Her reflection during the session is striking. She says: "He is on good terms with himself, he is *his own.*" She is clearly aware of this. Diana expresses her lack of a nucleus of stone and of an envelope that should contain her, within which a psychic movement of "counting on oneself" could be sketched.

The word *"suyo"* [his] was worked through in various contexts of meaning.

> A year later, the sequence of two dreams forms a landmark in Diana's analysis. Through the analysis of these dreams are profiled the beginnings of the construction of the nucleus of stone. At the same time, Diana begins to rid herself of her pathological envelopes (of suffering, toxicity, promiscuity), which are dissolving, to the patient's great surprise; she does not feel the imperious need to consume hallucinogens or compulsively to seek sexual partners. She begins to feel good about spending an evening alone at home, and she can concentrate on her studies.
>
> *The first dream*
>
> *"I am going by car with a man to a woman's house. We were looking for a house where that woman lived alone. We could not find the way, he went another way. 'Do you know where it is?' he said to me. 'You know where the supermarket is?' I replied. We arrived, and the house was very beautiful, fascinating, it appeared designed by an architect, and I had to go and look for a box, and to go by myself. I had to climb onto the roof . . . and I took hold of it, and when I turned around X was looking at me, he was playing a seduction game like when we meet at night in a snack-bar. I did not go off with him, I went off with the box."*
>
> Associations lead to the following representations: she associ-

ates the supermarket with a youth festival, with a first illusion that she liked a boy, who years later was to confess to her that he, too, had liked her. It was a happy period in her life, to be followed by some dark years. She said it was a period in which "I was not yet perverted".

The box refers to an artistic work that Diana has to carry out. She says: "The box has to stop being a box and become something virtually different. The form of a prism must disappear and turn into an illusion, a scenario." She also associates *caja* [box] with *caca* [shit]. The box thus becomes a valuable treasure, an esteemed gift.

The woman at whose house they arrive is a horrible woman, "without femininity or neatness, grey-haired". She associates her with the mother of a friend with whom she shared the bad years of her life.

"*Caja*" [box] appears as a significant key. In the dream Diana looks at X (a combined montage of many men with whom she has gone out), but finally she decides to go off alone with her box. The box is an identifying possession, it is the "private thing" that she is beginning to value, it is the representative of a transformation that is operating in it, linked with the installation of the place of stone. The box is her genitals, her house, her body, her creative power. An important work of discrimination is verified in Diana, who shows frequent episodes of indiscrimination, of fusion with the primal object in the exercise of her envelopes—toxic-pathological, concerned with suffering, or bodily and sensual. In the dream, the fascinating house of the grey-haired lady (the mother's home) is a condensation of this theme. The sinister aspect emerges in the image of that woman in the dream—a negative, bisexual figure. Diana is seeking, from her artistic outflowing, to build houses herself (in the analysis she is trying to build herself). In two associations there appears the figure of an architect—possibly an appeal to a constant organizing axis, the support and foundation of the psyche.

As Resnik (1990) writes, "Each body is a house, and the central column of this house is the father"—another reference to a central organizing axis.

According to Bleger (1967), the transformation that operates in Diana indicates a greater discrimination of the agglutinated nucleus—the psychotic part beginning to be converted into a neurotic part.

In heterosexual erotic transference, Diana needs me to take a masculine position and exert the paternal function.

> In one session she tells me that she has visited the house where she had spent her childhood. It is now occupied by others; but in the garden the great tree with a hefty trunk, which her grandfather planted, remains intact. This tree is an allusion to her genealogical tree, in which her identity comes into play, and represents in the cathexis of a branch-axis the matrix of the nucleus of stone whose psychic presence it is beginning to incorporate.

> *Second dream*

> A second dream, a few days after the first, confirms the process that is going on in Diana. It is only an image, a sketch, but on this apparently anodyne dream rich associations are poured out. Diana had the task of making a drawing by choosing an image and then making three transformations on it. She says: "*I chose a man's arm with feathers tattooed on it. In one it says 'Mother'. The rest of the arm has skin. The transformations I made consist of tracing the arm and moving the feathers down, filling the feathers with fingers, giving the whole thing the appearance of a skeleton.*" New associations lead to a search for firmness, for a basis of support. As has already been described, the place of stone slips in through allusions that semantically refer to a skeleton—support, framework, ownership, integrity.

> A certain feeling of estrangement appears weeks afterwards. Diana feels that something is changing, she feels fear—the fear of turning into a "normal person".

The change experienced by the patient implies passing from a psychic space in disorder, a chaos of confusion, to a space in which the nucleus of stone is producing structural psychic effects. She says:

> "... what I was talking about, that something is taking shape inside which gives rise to other things, like a skeleton. ... I have an urge to be alone. ... I could never say that ... since I am alone."

"To be" comes out as a privileged significance. The long silence that follows these words is conceptualized by me as a psychic moment of "being with oneself" in trophic solitude.

The psychic centre of gravity is gathering strength day by day. Already Diana does not need to enter compulsively into the confused hallucinatory world of drugs. She says:

> "Yesterday they offered me acid, and I had no wish to take anything, and I respected my wishes. ... Things are happening that aren't like things happening from outside, like me going with my little box (allusion to the box of the previous dream), and I say: 'I'm going with my little box, which is mine, I made it'."

In a later session she rejected my interventions. I respect her need to "throw me out" in order to go on arming her own space, alone, as though she needed a sort of "psychic exile" in the presence of her analyst and the essential came into play in the fact of being with herself. Diana is showing in her analysis the emergence of experiences in which "the different thing", "the new thing", "the thing never experienced before", signals the arrival of the nucleus of stone.

THE BODY OF AFFECT

Affect is the result of a complex metabolism, somato-psychic, sensorial, and instinctual, which establishes itself on the terrain of intersubjectivity. It occupies a place at a cross-roads that is a meeting-place for what might be called the "experiential mass"—a conglomeration of sensations, perceptions, circulation of energy, feelings—and where the erogenous also comes into play.

There is an affective memory, and in addition the affects are mounted on the various classifications of instincts: erotic affects, destructive affects, preservation affects, and so on. To a primal energy, seat of the first affects in the pleasure–unpleasure range, are added secondary affects (Green, 1970) or organized affects that can be named and defined. The affect is what circulates "between words", "before the word", like a fringe of what cannot be described and can be transmitted only through experience, of atmosphere, of climate, of subjective occurrences that continuously accompany the subject, "like pressure on the surface of the body" (Freud, 1895b).

The senses also carry affects. Pleasure and unpleasure constitute the basis of sensuality. Affect is converted into effect on the sensual body. Affects of vitality and categorical affects (Stern, 1985) form yet another classification. The vital affects constitute a certain form of experience, and through them an attempt is made to give names to numerous characteristics of the emotions that do not appear in the existing vocabulary or in the taxonomy of affects. These indescribable characteristics can be understood by means of dynamic, kinetic terms such as "to rise", "to evaporate", "fleeting", "explosive", "crescendo", "decrescendo", "to explode", "to stretch", and so forth. The different forms of emotion provoked by these vital processes affect the organism most of the time. They never abandon us, whether or not we are conscious of them. The categorical affects, unlike the vital affects, come and go.

Affects operate, therefore, in the field of the unformalizable (Sciarreta, personal communication). They are almost impossible to express, and they exist and circulate in the intimacy of bodies, in transmission without words. They are partly included in what Lacan calls "the real".

The body of affects throws out a challenge to the reconstruction of scenes. We arrive at the concept of affects as "psychic matrices" (Green, 1970, p. 17), as mute "emergences" that carry in their depths (now the attachment to the order of the representation becomes indispensable) whole fragments of a submerged history.

Freud writes (1916–17):

> What is an affect in the dynamic sense? It is in any case "*something highly composite*" [italics added]. An affect includes in the first place particular motor innervations or discharges and sec-

> ondly certain feelings; the latter are of two kinds—perceptions of the motor actions that have occurred and the direct feelings of pleasure and unpleasure which, as we say, give the affect its keynote. . . . We seem to see deeper in the case of some affects and to recognise that the core which holds the combination we have described together is the repetition of some particular significant experience. [pp. 395–396]

The affect submerged in the body, covering it like a cloak, sometimes keeps the legendary secrets of stories on a certain subject that pass from one generation to another.

Affect in all its richness and complexity appears like a new "via regia" through which filters the unnameable, that which is not yet incorporated in the order of speech, that which belongs to another order.

Freud said, "The emotional state . . . is always justified" (1900a, p. 75), even in the discord that joins it to its content. The body of affect implies an intrasubjectivity and an intersubjectivity, a dialogue of emotions with those beings who are "important to us" as we go through life. It is a humanized instinctual body on which the emotions, the sentiments of the other significant things, inscribe marks that are predominantly erotic or destructive and will even determine possibilities of health or illness between the sensitive body and the somatic body.

The erogenous body is intimately interwoven with the body of affect. The first seeks society, specific action, satisfaction of the sexual appetite, discharge, use of an object to achieve its end. Sometimes this erogenous body is used as a defensive screen to suppress or choke intense affective experiences. The body of affect is very near to it. Rooted in ancient emotions, it is a body of constant interchange with its fellows, a body of omnipotence and helplessness, of communication, which comes into contact with another body that is sensitive to the effects that a definite representation exerts on it: one word makes a tear fall, another hardens the expression, yet another generates a wave of voluptuousness. Biology gives way to the speaking subject, and sensuality becomes more complex. The country of affects is not simple; and thus a blow may bring order and a caress constitute a violent act, the product of a pathological sexual overstimulation.

Sometimes the erogenous body is at the service of the protection of a fellow being. The appearance is erotic: behind the body is pure affect, on the altars of self-preservation (as we shall see in the case of Mary—in this chapter—who in imagination offers her virginity with the intention of thus "saving" the life of a friend). The erogenous body obtains a suffering pleasure (unpleasure for the erogenous body, satisfaction for the psyche, which experiences the fact of giving up its body as a heroic deed).

The erogenous body unites with psychic pain and offers itself as the object for reparation. It is a body gained for suffering with the aim of maintaining life (one's own or that of a loved one).

The body emerges as a gift, as a possible offering. Different orders of body-to-body are outlined: words (voice as body), gestures, tender caresses (instincts finally restricted), uninhibited sensuality, violence. To the direct body-to-body is added a body of which an intention is the mediator. Now the body is an object of use, an interested interchange; it requires a profit, it is exploited, it is put into conditions outside the spectrum of pleasure or enjoyment. It is a body that looks for revenge, to make money, to achieve power and dominate any situation, a body that "knows" about the body. The affect is not only a narcissistic sex-instinct; behind it is the idea of self-preservation and the preservation of others, by protecting, feeding, and caring for them, and the recreation or rebuilding of object-relations.

Affect may mark the body in ways that are transient and fleeting, or ways that may occur insistently, constantly. Wrinkles, gestures, curvatures, radiances, and so on give the game away to ourselves and anyone who watches us or reads us and can interpret these signals according to his own affective and representational code.

The body of affect consists of repressed unconscious and conscious components. Together with Joyce McDougall (1989), I want to point out the defensive importance of the disaffected body in a subject who has decided to avoid emotions and is seeking a pacifying indifference.

The body of affect is primarily a body of energy and magnetism, sometimes positive, sometimes negative. It is a body that generates responses and constitutes a pattern that is voiceless but at the same time intensely alive and present in the field of interminable human interchanges. It can show positive affects (stimulating, life-giving, protective) and negative affects (death-bringing, destructive).

There is a first body of affect, conceived in the mists of time—a body desired to a greater or lesser extent, a body on the way to narcissization, a body of pain and satisfaction, of extreme omnipotence and helplessness, the first human body prepared for access to language. The primitive bodily ego receives and emits the various primal affective trends that interact with the instinctual field and with the field of the senses.

The erogenous body, mounted on the body of affect, reveals the dimension of human love.

The "body-to-body" of affect in an analysis

Affects appear—sometimes manifestly, sometimes hidden—in the experience of transference in analysis, in a form that can reveal, know intuitively, and even invent, according to the analyst's power to make the connection, from unconscious to unconscious, with the internal world of his patient. To talk about "affect" is to bring the body into play. All affect is a centrifugal process directed towards the interior of the body, and "this unchaining is for the body what motor discharges are for the external world" (Green, 1970, p. 46). Affect in its quality as "motor" and "secretive" indicates how intimately it is anchored to the somatic body.

When Green says, "what refers to the analyst cannot be other than affect" (1970, p. 67), affect brings us back to a body touched in its living matter by humanized flesh. The body touched by affect indicates a new path for sensuality: it is that of *affective sensuality*. The constructions (Freud, 1937d) aim to evoke buried scenes and make affects blossom in their varied range (anxiety, pain, mourning, depersonalization, annihilation, hate, joy, etc.) until they touch the limit of the nameable in the register of affects as we approach the realm of the unutterable and irrepresentable, that which is without representational link but whose efficacy makes us feel its effects, which can perhaps be confronted and manifested only in the gestation of the affective field between analyst and analysand. In this field there comes into play a power of transmission that is outside the word, and we have the capacity to guess (however inadequate our words may be) the patient's *senti* (D. Anzieu, 1970) and to work regressively through the successive hypothetical happenings that may underlie the conscious or unconscious affective atmosphere.

In trying to read these experiences of reality in an analysis, we are carrying out a task of symbolization and dealing with the *handwriting of the body of affect* that every patient inevitably exposes to us.

The body of affect appears to us with its discords, its defences, its suppressions, displacements, conversions, and transformations. In its interrelation with the erogenous body, it lets us see the organic repressions (Freud, 1930a) that have established themselves on it.

The body of affect is a living presence in analytic work, and the cure will depend—to some extent—on the changes in the "effective body" or "field of desire" or "field of mutual transmission or divination" between those two subjects who battle body-to-body in the work of making the unconscious conscious. The capacity of the analyst to "feel with" and to "feel against" is crucial to letting suppressed affects emerge and daring to break into affective archaisms (envy, jealousy, hate, love . . .). It will be necessary to interact with them in an ever-changing force-field in which *Eros* and *Thanatos* spend a long time fighting for supremacy.

Mary's pain

Didier Anzieu writes (1985, ch. 16): "Pain is not the opposite or the reverse of pleasure; its relationship is asymmetrical. Satisfaction is an 'experience', suffering is a 'test'."

For Mary, all her childhood was a long test of survival, an intense struggle to bear the pain in her body of affect. Early on, her body had been hurt by negative affects at qualitative and quantitative levels. She could not establish a primary identification with a support-object to which she could have clung, she had no reassuring representations "of possessing a common skin with the support-object maintained" (D. Anzieu, 1985, p. 99).

As the container function of the skin-ego failed her, there emerged diffuse, unlocatable anxieties or emptiness anxieties corresponding to what Anzieu conceptualized as a filtering skin-ego, which lacks the aggressiveness necessary for any self-affirmation.

In Didier Anzieu's words (1985): "One of the main nuclei of the ego consists of the image-sensation of an internal phallus, maternal or more generally paternal, which assures for the mental space in process of constitution a first axis, of the order of verticality and of struggle against weight, and which prepares for the experience of one's own psychic life" (p. 98).

Mary's legend of birth was inauspicious. By "legend of birth" I understand the manifest story of the parents' desires with regard to the future human person and the situation in which she apparently made her entry into the world.

Mary's father, a foreigner, had emigrated, leaving in his own country two daughters about whom he did not want to know. He married Mary's mother on the *sine qua non* condition that they should avoid having children. Mary's mother was fertile and had many abortions. In Mary's case—as her own mother told me in an interview before I made the acquaintance of my patient—confusing losses of blood with menstruation, she arrived at the fourth month of pregnancy, when abortion is already dangerous, and she persuaded the father to let her have this child. A certain wish for maternity played a part in the mother (and perhaps also in the father). The story goes that the father, not resigned to his lot, punched the mother in the abdomen with the intention that she should lose her future child. According to another story, the father took the mother on a high-speed motorcycle ride on a road full of potholes, with the intention of causing an abortion.

Mary was born despite the blows. The wishes of both parents for prenatal death were conscious. She was intended to die with the other foetuses, her siblings. Researches in foetal psychology describe foetal responses to signs of violence, and Bowlby (1980) insists on the importance of going sensorially into the selection, interpretation, and evaluation of what is stored in the memory. Mary's affective memory *knew* no happiness, nor security, and her embryonic body was castigated with words and blows.

As usually happens with adolescent rebellion, once the child transgresses and triumphs over them, the parents accept it. By being born alive and healthy, Mary had committed her first transgression. Through her normal birth Mary triumphed for the first time over death and unwittingly made reparation for her parents' death-wishes.

The defects in the skin-ego in its two variables—covering and penetration (Anzieu, 1985, based on the texts of Fisher and Cleveland)—are evident. Mary suffered from pathological, rigid envelopes, protecting herself in coverings of suffering (Enriquez, quoted by D. Anzieu, 1985), and she suffered from pathological penetrations (described as wound–fracture–bleeding–flattening) in the destructive violence exerted on her body in gestation or the blows inflicted on her in her childhood. Other envelopes, permeable, fragile and unconscious, accounted for her inability to defend herself against aggression and for the experience of not being able to contain and organize her thoughts and her affects (frequent tears, "unconscious" in that she could not associate them with any obvious reason for weeping), referring to the concept of the filtering skin-ego.

The pre-verbal, infralinguistic body (D. Anzieu, 1985) emerged in the sessions. The internalization of an affective knot (the analyst as support-object) in the form of a link experienced as unalterable and forever was fundamental if Mary was to repair her skin-ego little by little and find in her inner world the balancing centre of gravity essential in order to cease to be a survivor and begin to live.

Let us observe more closely the pathological covering that formed successively over Mary. Her parents had confined her in a forced cohabitation. She had begged them (she remembers it was when she was 10 to 12 years old) to give her a room of her own in their large house. She begged in vain. She had to witness the primal scene, even though she wrapped herself in a blanket and plugged her ears so as not to hear the moans and words that the parents exchanged during their sexual relations.

Like Bowlby (1980) we can speak of an "unspeakable misery" —a misery that Mary begins to narrate, suffering intense feelings of pain in repeating the difficult moments of her life. A certain quantum of affect cannot be put into words: it is with sighs, prolonged silences, and diffuse and unforeseen anxiety that she gives an account of the "unspeakable" part of her suffering.

She remembers that in the fullness of the oedipal stage she would conceal her emotions as she waited for affective recognition of her father towards her. She felt only that she was receiving indifference. Her father came back from work in a bad temper and immediately went to bed; his meal was served to him in bed. Mary was obliged to eat in the same room, at a desk, "with her legs striking against the drawers, in an uncomfortable position". Her body was confined, as she had to obey a quietness that was far from the uproar of *Eros*. Mary suffered and organized masochistic fixations. She seemed condemned to live with little psychic space for her needs and desires. She remembers the anxiety, she felt in experiencing a visceral, primal affect, a sort of emptiness anxiety, when faced with the abandonment of which she was the object.

Her parents' sexuality is described as "abusive". She remembers parties in the house, with her mother heavily made up, the object of the gaze of other men who "chased her around the house".

The original phantasies are presented to her in a negative aspect. We have already seen how the phantasy of intra-uterine life was tinged with blood and blows and murderous desires (leaving behind the dreamed-of paradise of being wrapped up in the mother's body). The primal scene tortured her in her first childhood. We shall soon see how castration and seduction are linked.

Seduction was carried out by a sinister personage—a bricklayer with whom her mother left her alone, delivered up to an aggressive sexuality. This man took off her skirt and touched her. Pleasure, confusion, shame, and fear were the affects aroused by this repeated experience. The bricklayer built a pool at the bottom of the garden—a pool without "defences", which was a metaphor for the feeling of having no sufficient reassuring trophic bodily limit.

In that pool, Mary's castration phantasy was to be played out through the death of a child. This little boy, Carlos, who could scarcely walk yet—Mary's symbolic brother—lived next-door. There was no fence between the houses, and the little boy spent most of the time with Mary's mother; together, they bathed and fed him. Once again there emerges the picture of a mother who abandons and kills, in the person of Carlos's mother and Mary's own mother. One fateful afternoon, Mary saw Carlos going to the bottom of the garden. Some time afterwards, Mary's mother asked for him. He had drowned in the pool. "I saw him born—I was five years old", she was to weep in the session years later. The first corpse, the first death to give new meaning to her aborted foetal siblings, which fixed in her "the guilt of being alive". Although I believe it is more suitable to emphasize that it was not so much a question of "living" as of "surviving", in that her psychic life was crushed and oppressed by a multitude of little corpses that made marks of intense pain on her body.

The first years of Mary's childhood were spent in this "climate of negative affect". Didier Anzieu writes (1985): "One learns to love bitterness, one sees oneself more or less obliged to pay attention to unpleasant experiences. From intersubjectivity there is created a cruel imperative of the superego and a facilitation of masochism."

This only child was, some time later, to call herself "the survivor".

Mary's adolescence went a little better. She was a good student and began to have friends and freedom. But in an almost demonic repetition, when she was 17 she consulted a gynaecologist, and he seduced her. The scene she describes is pathetic: he took her to a couch and ordered her to keep quiet. Then he raped and deflowered her. A climate of phantasy appears to hang over this scene when it is put into words in the sessions. Mary was a member of a student organization, and a friend, probably missing (truth or fiction: she herself does not know), had to be saved. The doctor may have indicated a way of salvation. Mary, in her phantasy, had sacrificed her virginity, offering her body to save another. This is part of her basic dramatics: to repair and resuscitate the dead, to expiate her guilt because life had been her lot while so many foetuses–children–young people were lying dead.

During the scene with the doctor, the erogenous body was transformed into a body of preservation for another. The scenes took on a new meaning, and Mary still seemed to be used, sacrificed to others' desire for death, expelled from herself.

In her body she had expressed this intolerance to life with fainting fits at school, which expressed a sort of hysterical weakness when faced with her companions. Also, frequent attacks of bronchitis obliged her to spend many winter days shut up at home with a high fever (envelope of heat?).

Shortly afterwards, on losing the friend she also called Carlos, like the child who died in the pool, Mary made her first suicide attempt. She was 18 years old. She took barbiturates. To leave the hostile world was her most vehement desire. Again there was an erotic repetition: life was waiting for her, and her mother arrived in time to save her.

A little later she began a love affair with Adolfo, and both of them began treatment with the same therapist. Adolfo also treated her badly, as did her therapist who, after a holiday break, informed her that he no longer considered her his patient, and he went on treating Adolfo.

On one occasion Adolfo said to her that with her madness it would be impossible for her to be a good mother and to nurse children.

A little later she made another attempt at suicide, this time trying to gas herself in the kitchen. The olfactory envelope would be there to protect her, to take her to a better world. By a fortunate repetition the mother came with a "breath of life" to this daughter destined to live. Mary was saved again. The sado-masochistic climate in her couple relationship increased until they ended by separating.

At that time Mary was 21 years old. Her mother looked for a new therapist for her, and so came to me. That was 13 years ago.

Fragments of Mary's analysis and observations

When Mary's mother asked me for an interview, her first demand was that I should be her accomplice in a lie. She had chosen me from a list at a medical agency, but her daughter was to believe that a doctor well known to the family had given her my name. I doubted whether to take her on, in view of the seriousness of her violent attempts at suicide, which her mother had described to me.

I then made an appointment with Mary, and immediately I felt that it was appropriate to begin the work of analysis. I wondered what qualities of excitation had inscribed on Mary's body of affect a memory so painful that she had to "kill with her death".

The analysis lasted for about seven years, without interruption. During the first two month-long holidays she had sessions with another analyst, on my recommendation. Mary had a great capacity for insight and a very great wish to explore her inner world. It was fundamental during the treatment to go back to pre-oral stages to try to re-establish, in the reassuring analyst–analysand atmosphere, the broken limits and the damaged body of affect by stimulating the integrative impulse of the ego (Luquet, quoted by Anzieu, 1985) through the analytic work. Without a doubt, the masochistic suffering was eroticized.

How can one give a brief account of all the unconscious affects that took place over the course of time? I have chosen significant fragments of various sessions, and then a sequence of two sessions during an important crisis in the middle of her analysis.

Let us listen to Mary:

> "We are born in order to live. . . . I do not feel that I have lived all this time, I was not free, it was like being shut inside my belly."
>
> "I was born in summer. People were dying of heat. While others were dying, I gave myself the luxury of being born."
>
> "I feel that I have been killing myself a lot, and I cannot go on like this."
>
> "I am too fond of maltreating myself."
>
> "Papa once spat in my face—I was 14 years old—because the manager in him said to me, 'What do you think of those men?' I said to him, 'They're all pigs'. Then he insulted me from top to bottom, spat at me, and wanted to kill me with a revolver, he began to clean the revolver, loaded it, I lay down on the bed and Mother stood in the doorway of my room. 'See where that filth is that doesn't deserve to live', said my father."
>
> "I think that I can't do anything, I can't erase everything I have experienced, I can't bear it, I can't."
>
> "One day when I was a little girl I had a fright that depressed me. I was disgusted by ox-tongue, and when Mother cooked tongue she told me when she had already finished cleaning it,

and one day she said to me, 'here it is', and I peeped, and she came with the tongue, saying to me 'Ugh!' and now I laughed, but I was very frightened."

In July 1984 we worked on a dream: *"It is in a house in the quarter where she lived in her childhood. There is a fence around the house. Going out, she left a coat behind. There was a guy inside, and she could not go in because of that guy."* She associates with the coat, that "it is something I like and I left it there". I point out to her that there are hidden things [*tapado* = coat; *tapar* = to cover, conceal] that do not let her live, which we shall go and see.

A.M.A.: My hypothesis is that you have seen things that you do not want to remember. Or that you experienced them.

MARY: Probably. It has to be something very ugly, which stains. There was a tin with something very ugly. A feeling of something rotten. After that I did not want to open another tin. It was something that we had never bought. Sausages.

A.M.A.: Possibly these memories have something to do with sexual facts, and here we do not talk very much about sex.

MARY: For me sex is not bad. In my family it is. In my view they did ugly things with sex.

A perverse, promiscuous envelope formed part of the pathological envelope of Mary's life.

One night in January 1984 Mary left a call for help on my telephone answering machine, saying in a weak voice that she felt a desire to kill herself.

I arrived home late that night, listened to the call, and as she had no telephone at home, I could not phone her back. On the following morning, as I knew her address, I went to her house. Mary lived alone. Her emotion on seeing me was great. I stayed and talked to her for a few minutes, long enough to see that she could hold out until the following session, and then I left.

* * *

Let us now look at a fragment of a session in September 1984, before another crisis.

MARY: My grandmother pinched her children with pliers, once because one had eaten a peach that was for my grandfather. She tortured them to make them confess, and made them kneel in a corner, in maize. When she died, she must have been good, although not as good as all that, because she once threw a child into the dustbin.

A.M.A.: You also ran the risk of falling into a dustbin before you were born. How can you live with these stories on your back?

MARY: I remember something: I see myself weeping, and I tighten my skirt.

A.M.A.: Perhaps you feel that nobody protected you from the men who might have touched you or taken your skirt off.

MARY [*assents—short silence*]: Besides, every time I feel bad it's also so that my mother will take care of me. . . . I have had more playthings in my life than any other little girl. And what for? I had nobody to play with. Every time I wanted to kill myself, I took different steps, and so it was, I think, like being enraged because they were nasty to me, I became very sad, and afterwards it came upon me that I want to punish them . . . they have to suffer like me.

A.M.A.: With your death.

MARY: Yes, and afterwards I think . . . what does it matter to them about me . . . nobody cares what is happening to me.

A.M.A.: And does love sustain you?

MARY: There is no love. There is no love at all. And I go on doing things quickly.

A.M.A.: What things?

MARY: Well, things . . . searching, thinking how to do it. . . . I think of various things . . . first taking tablets, then knowing that they did not work . . . then something else . . . not stabbing myself, because that will hurt, it has to be something I won't be sorry about. [*Laughs*]

A.M.A.: What you want is to kill something that is not letting you live, or to fulfil an order of your parents who thought of killing you before you were born, though it didn't matter too much to them that you lived. But the one it matters to is you.

MARY: And I stopped because I thought: somebody minds what happens to me . . . as if I had somebody to help me—do you understand?

A.M.A.: I represent the Mary with a desire for life, with strength, and hidden treasure; then there are not only painful things, but also a potential for joy. What is more, I believe that you have felt concretely that I am concerned about you; it was important when I was at your house.

Mary: Yes, I was thinking about that recently. Then I thought: she minds what happens to me. It was a complete revelation that day, it was as though I felt the same, you know, as when we were at college, when we followed the flag—we moved off holding each other by the belt, and I felt, as it were, the mistress's hand . . . following the flag.

A.M.A.: We shall follow the flag.

On Friday of this same week there was another crisis; she took a low dose of barbiturates. It was her mother who called me. Mary had said to her on the telephone: "Now I am going to kill myself and you are going to suffer." I spoke with Mary on the telephone, she wept in anguish: "It's because Mother went to bed with that man."

A.M.A.: That is something you were keeping hidden, and so you had to say it.

MARY: It disgusts me.

A.M.A.: We have to remember it in order to be able to forget it.

We saw each other again on the following day.

Following session:

MARY: I remember this chap who was so much in the house, he was called J, and he came to do plastering or the plumbing. . . . I talked to Mother about what we saw in an earlier session about the skirt, and I asked whether A, the maid, went with this chap. She told me no. "Well," I said to her, "I am going to remember anyway". And I shut up. Later she said to me: "What do you have to remember?" And I was very frightened of the form of that question, palpitations suddenly seized me and made me very afraid. I don't know if anything was going to happen that would have frightened me.

A.M.A: Would it not be that you were going to see your father with that girl?

MARY: No. I don't know. As regards A, when I was going off to school she made him come. The day I had been frightened because there was a festival and a friend of Father's went with my mother and I began to cry, I was very afraid . . . that has nothing to do with the feelings I have. . . . I don't know; I left it there. . . . on Friday morning I awoke with the feeling that it was my mother. . . . I don't know if I had dreamed something or . . . and I remembered that she had put me to bed for the siesta, she put me on Father's side and sang me to sleep. I woke up. Mother was not there, and I was actually in the room opposite, where the maid slept. There was a big bed with two places, that was where I was to sleep after that, and then I got up very quickly, I got as far as the door, and I can't remember what happened after that, and afterwards I ran out to the yard and then that chap came to find me . . . the one from the yard, I remembered him from before, crouching like that, he had a V-neck sweater, he was smiling to me—a cruel sun—and I was certain that it had been my mother who had been with him, and I felt that I was going to go mad . . . it was the first time that anything like that had happened to me.

A.M.A.: [*I go back to the latent part of the dream and tell her that we are beginning to uncover those things which do not let her live.*]

MARY: Yes, I felt on very bad terms with my mother, on Friday I did not work, she came to bring me various things, I did not want to see her. . . .

A.M.A.: Do you remember that you called her and told her that you were going to kill yourself?

MARY: Yes, at that moment I didn't give Mother a kiss. She went away at once, I didn't say anything to her, I was terrified of telling her . . . great fear. . . . I said it to Adolfo, and I felt worse because it was as though now I had said that, I had to die.

A.M.A.: As punishment?

MARY: Yes.

A.M.A.: Have you wanted to kill that chap more than once?

MARY: Yes, of course.

A.M.A.: And what you want to kill now are those memories.

MARY: Yes, and afterwards I felt I was going to kill myself, but I did not die, I was quiet as if I had been separated from the body of what I thought, and I did not do anything. She should never have left me by myself so that nothing could happen to me, I should have died as a child, to teach her that a child should not be left alone.

A.M.A.: Like Carlos?

MARY: Yes, after what happened with Carlos [*deep sigh*] . . . yes, while we're on the subject, I let him go off, I saw him going towards the pool. . . .

A.M.A.: *You* have felt guilty at being alive since you were born, since you were six years old, for ever.

MARY: Yes.

At the end of this session, I explain to her the underlying lie in the derivation—as though it were the moment to cast light also on what is "hidden" in our initial link.

Here I leave the observation of Mary. Six years have already passed since the end of her analysis. She has settled in a small town by the sea. She has bought a house with a beautiful garden. On two occasions she has travelled, and has had a series of sessions of re-analysis. Not long ago she wrote to me to announce that "for my delight" (and hers, certainly) she is living with someone and is very happy.

GIVING ONESELF A BODY, SHARING BODIES

With the title "giving oneself a body", I am deliberately leaving aside the expression "object-finding" as usually used in psychoanalysis in order to emphasize the living materiality of the bodily presence of a fellow being and its incidence in psychic reality, in the sense of the German *Nebenmensch* [*neben:* near, *Mensch:* person], which expresses the position of nearness of one person to another.

All through life, bodies interact. Bodily contacts organize the psyche, feeding it with experiences of relationships. Not only is it important to be touched; just as important is the context in which the touching takes place. To the quantity and the quality of sensorial interchange is added the dimension of the desire that is present.

The first body-to-body contact takes place with the mother–woman–housewife, the bearer of the "preferred form". The vulnerable infant clings to her sweet anatomy, her milky breasts, her enveloping, nourishing, and protecting body. This body, the primal source of security, also appears as bisexual, combined. The *infans* responds to this body-to-body by desiring to complete the mother, imagining itself as a phallus (Lacan, 1958) at the appropriate time. The preferred form stamps on the body of the infant the first *senti* (D. Anzieu, 1970) and exerts upon it the first necessary violence (Aulagnier, 1975); it generates upon it the first "primordial orgasms" (Alizade, 1989).

The first significant other makes of the body the support on which the infant traces its own body, composes its corporal unity by removing the phantasy of a "body torn apart", recognizes its bodily frontiers, defines its inside and its outside, and supposes itself to be sexed. Spitz (1965) has studied the principal role played by this first body, and the risk run by a baby when it lacks it (at the extreme are the cases of marasmus, which he describes so poignantly).

An interesting aspect to consider is the condition of "sharing bodies" that is inherent in the space between bodies marked out by existence. Right from the start we have to talk about this first body-to-body with the mother, the peremptory function that comes from a primal object, which will have to withdraw from the enchantment of the dyad to give way to triangulation. No body can possess itself completely. To be excluded from the mother's dyad and to have to "learn to share" what is loved becomes a means of constructing functions for the psychic apparatus.

The category of being human implies a perpetual interaction with one's fellows (be they real, imaginary, or symbolic). The human person is made out of the vicissitudes of various contacts—sensorial, identifying, affective, and so on. It is formed as a mirror-image of its fellow beings, from the play of identification and non-identification, in the absorption of psychic heritages. It gives shape to the unconscious image of the body (Dolto, 1984), "the unconscious symbolic incarnation of the desiring subject", which, interwoven with the bodily schema, enables communication with fellow beings.

The conformation of the skin-ego (D. Anzieu, 1985) and autoerotic experiences on the body delimit that ineffable feeling of being "unique" that is the basis of identification. The parents' narcissism spills onto the incipient being, to the advantage of the size of its ego (Freud, 1914c)—that is to say, an increase in its self-esteem. When puberty commences and the adolescent begins his exogamic movement, there appears on his horizon the search for, and discovery of, the object. The child's "receiving a body" is exchanged for "giving oneself a body". The body of the fellow being, even when ephemeral, becomes a necessary, essential object, both in the realm of phantasy and in that of reality. Thus ". . . an object or a being begins to exist for us by desire or by love" (Merleau-Ponty, 1945, p. 171). "Giving oneself a body" is transformed into a *vital function*. It implies going in search of other beings and using one's body for pleasure, enjoyment, and love, in a way that is either transitory or more or less durable.

In body-to-body situations the range of instincts comes into play, with one or other instinct predominating, according to each individual case. The instinct of attachment (Bowlby, 1969) is shown in the need to count on the presence of another body as a surface to contact, that which produces well-being and a feeling of pleasure. The instinct of contrectation is expressed (Moll, quoted by Freud, 1905c) in the peremptory instinctual need to establish "contact" with the beings surrounding us. The instinct of self-preservation crops up when the presence of the object guarantees, in addition to sexual satisfactions, the survival of that subject in its immediate material aspects.

Giving oneself a body is a constant daily manifestation in which *Eros* plays its part, but in which *Thanatos* also is present. When it predominates, it is the alien body looking towards destruction, the perverted body-to-body. The instinct to dominate seeks in its turn the possession of the object and imposes on it submission, if not servitude. At other times the body will accept being the corporal depository of the "leavings" of another body.

The dimension of the sublime is not lacking in body-to-body situations. At this point there operates a fraction of instinct diverted from its sexual end which "raises the object to the dignity of the Thing" (Lacan, 1959–1960). There can be an ethical element amid the clamour of sexual interchange.

* * *

The erogenous body of the fellow being may be desired totally or partially. In the first case it is a question of amorous friendship, of falling in love, or of true love. The body, opening to a fellow being, opens to his or her history, memories, mnemonic traces. Psychic intimacy accompanies the intimacy of flesh, and the combination of the two intensifies the quality of pleasure. The relationship is one of pleasure/love.

When the erogenous body is sought only in partial form, for its capacity to give pleasure, it is a question of trying to keep the benefits of that erogenous body maintained in the time of desire. The relationship is one of pleasure/desire. This is the sphere of the kerb-crawler, the prostitute, the man-object. What is striven for is a satiation of the senses and the experience of pleasing with the least possible affective commitment. The prostitute is an extreme example of this. Anonymity adorns her. She is required to be unknown, devoid of all passion, and expert in the art of giving pleasure, of making the erogenous zones bring out their maximum pleasurable capacity. She is a professional of the erogenous techniques and declares herself free of the barriers of organic repression.

As affect increases eroticism, we can see in some cases (the expert in the arts of pleasing knows this well) the artificial search for affect in the frame of "verse", in the false promises of love that seek only the increase of sensual ardour.

Erogenous bodily interchange is tied up with illusory or transitional space (Winnicott, 1953), potentiating play effects that enable the unfolding of trophic narcissistic phantasies. Then once more there shines in the encounter "His or her Majesty . . ."—paraphrasing the Freud of 1915—in the field of narcissism. It is a question of the majesty of subjects united in the revitalizing bodily adventure. The narcissistic expansion of falling in love opens out a magnetic terrain in which ecstasy shows its face. James Joyce conveys this idea in the words he puts into Molly Bloom's mouth in *Ulysses.* Her "Yes", repeated many times, proclaims the nearness of surrender, of the lovers' meeting, and points to the moving joy that is felt on sharing a pact of intimacy with a fellow being. It is not only the bodies that tell of their burning desire, but the psyches that repeat it. The "yes" is set going and widens the spectrum of vital interchange. Everything seems possible: routine and daily frustration are forgotten. The magic certainty of complete love is glimpsed on the horizon.

Let us listen to Molly:

> And then I asked him with my eyes to ask again yes and then he asked me would I yes . . . and first I put my arms around him yes and drew him down to me so he could feel my breasts all perfume yes and his heart was going like mad and yes I said yes I will yes.

Because to give oneself a body is to give oneself a sensorial envelope and a psychic envelope; meanwhile the "other" brings trophic elements, now at the level of self-preservation, now at the sensorial level of stimulation and discharge.

Finally, two main functions stand out in the exercise of body-to-body: (1) the function of obtaining pleasure (with or without the participation of possession) and (2) the supportive function of psychism (love and protection).

The pleasure function presents a facet of "rejuvenation" that is closely related to the biological bases. It consists of making the erogenous body work, of solving the problem of the process of discharge as though sexual life were a natural tonic, refreshing and revitalizing the somatic body, stimulating the secretion of hormones and their circulation. The presence of the object, by expelling every sign of present neurosis, sets up a field of participation for which the acquiescence of both participants is required. At this point we must not forget the ambivalence that may appear regarding all cathectization concerning the body. Aulagnier (1975) introduced the term "radical hate" to designate a violent emotion, rooted in the archaisms that are revived when a feeling of necessity towards one's fellow being is experienced. This "radical hate" appears when the body to which the individual reaches out as a source of instinctual gratification moves away or rejects the desire and chooses another erogenous–affective body. Hate is shown similarly when the encounter is ended, but with reservations, putting limits to the preliminary play and restricting in this way the partner's opportunity of reaching higher levels of pleasure. In the most trivial encounter of pure pleasure the subject is immersed in his world of phantasies, which interact in the field of the erogenous scene while it unfolds. A gesture, an attitude, an apparently anodyne word may change the erotic atmosphere, either in its favour or otherwise.

When the inclusion of enjoyment is added to the pleasure function, the death instinct comes into play. Into the regressional field of the encounter (see chapter three) comes depersonalization, the decathectization of the other as a different subject. And the other's body will be a mere pretext for going back along the road of consciousness and dodging the irrepresentable. The identifying play, the many personages that might have been projected into the chosen other one begin to withdraw. It is the moment of the exile of the personages, of the dissolution of the primal element, of the purely sensual body embraced in its entirety by the death instinct. What comes from the other is an archaic remnant, a babble of sounds, a rubbing of membranes, a rubbing of naked mucosae, in the stripping away of all precision, in the anarchy and disturbance of the erogenous zones. The real and the dimension of the indescribable filter through. Sensations, affects, images, vital rhythms, voluptuous waves resound.

Death appears—but this is death in the midst of life, death comparable to a dream, that is to say an experience approaching Nirvana, with the full knowledge that we have to return from this temporary state in a life-giving resurrection.

Bataille (1957) makes a distinction between the eroticism of bodies, the eroticism of hearts, and sacred eroticism. To the first he attributes a more egotistic and superficial character: it is cheap pleasure. In the eroticism of hearts, love, companionship, the highest values are added. Into sacred eroticism enters the attribute of God, of high ideals, of veneration and the sublime. Eroticism in capital letters implies a mixture of all three. The category of God, of the highest, is embodied in the exchange of love, respect, and gratitude. One step further is the body as a gift, as an offering—the magnanimous and generous handing over that recalls death and at the same time exorcism, which brings into the present a space of delights in which one body floods the other to forget pain, to seek refuge from intolerable reality. There is nothing better than a loving body surface to calm the anxiety of living, to make up for the drama of successive deficiencies with which existence confronts every subject. The erotic covering is like a veil that covers the body, protecting it from the wind and weather of life.

The function of giving oneself a body shows various shades, ranging from the degraded and perverse to the most sublime.

Another function of "giving oneself a body" is the function of support: support for love, support for protection. The body of one's fellow being moves close to one's own, to care for it, to protect it. The calming double element capable of installing itself between two people produces an experience of having a skin in common with another, or one body for two, which contributes to the imaginary re-establishment of the dyad with the primal object.

It can be said that it is not good for a human being to be alone. His human condition impels him to find himself bodies: sensual body, body of love (of direct satisfaction or sublimation}, body of friendship, of daily interchange, the fraternal body of a fellow-traveller.

The support function of "asking it of another body" offers a very interesting aspect when the subject has to face the crises of age and perceives his ageing. Each one will confront the situation as best he can, and some men will seek a younger wife, who can make them forget their own age and give the lie to the nearness of death (and vice versa). The youth of the other body is a great good, which the subject tries to appropriate through a mechanism that imitates "magic by contact".

Kawabata (1969) tells the story of a house in which beautiful young women are sleeping in rooms that old men rent, only to lie by the side of one of the young women and at most to touch her gently and nourish themselves on the presence of serene youth. The equations sleeping–tranquil–beautiful and death–youth are tranquillizing metonyms of a future re-encounter with the mother in the tomb, and above all they enable these old men to imagine a sweet death without fear and without mourning.

All sharing of bodies trophically includes room for sublimation. Sublimated eroticism is expressed in tenderness, in shared interests, in residual friendship beyond erotic attraction.

In "sharing bodies", we have to consider the time after the meeting, when the other body withdraws, and there comes the interval of temporary separation or final parting. What remains? A sound, the echo of a certain caress, bringing back to life yesterday's voluptuousness, the promise of future moments of pleasure and enjoyment, or a bitter taste. The value that each person puts on an "erogenous bodily act" intervenes here.

When the movement between bodies is predominantly erotic, in the sense that the life instincts dominate, then this vital quality permits that when a separation comes, of whatever type this may be, what has been sublimated will persist. The hate and destruction derived from natural human ambivalence is neutralized by this sublimatory trend and by the impulses restricted in its end.

And even in the case of a definitive separation, where an erotic link has existed, traumatic emotions can be minimized by human love—that is, love in its widest sense, a love beyond the mere narcissism of falling in love.

The subject in the midst of a separation will be able to face it less painfully if he has internalized a structure of care, an internal object-body in a sort of "intrapsychic maternalization", which brings with it an intrasubjective state of "being with" even when alone. The representations linked with the original phantasies will receive less negative charge—there will be less jealousy in the face of a potential primal scene, less desolation in the face of the castration anxiety underlying the loss of the attachment of the other body in loving interchange. Similarly, one can have confidence in being able to recover the lost object or to find an adequate substitute. The imaginary "cloister of the womb" constructed with the other in the fusion of symbiotic nuclei, or from the more highly evolved phantasy of "one skin for two", can be reconstructed. As far as seduction is concerned, wounded narcissism will tolerate its failure without too much harm to self-esteem.

The compulsion to the "other body"

Observation of Ophelia

Ophelia, a young analysand, is in despair at the feeling that she cannot maintain a love-relationship. To take to herself a body in a state of eroticism is an urgent necessity for her. She thus wraps her skin-ego in another skin, which serves her as a boundary and from which at the same time she expects her narcissistic confirmation as an object of love. Her body is wrapped to the full in excitation (A. Anzieu, 1987) springing from hysteria.

Giving herself a body emerges as a search for a psychic structure through succeeding in obtaining the narcissistic trophic charge, which allows her to mend the wounds in her skin-ego.

Under her apparent promiscuity there lies an impossible yearning for a meeting with a non-existent ideal. Experiences of love are therefore intense but ephemeral. While falling in love, she has feelings of ecstasy—she believes that at last she has found the perpetual object. As Azzeo (1991) writes: ". . . love at first sight ensures eternity through narcissistic magic and the father's immortality". In the shattering that follows the abandonment of the object we can see her intense masochistic fixations.

"Then I shall never have one!" she exclaims, referring to a possible couple. The resonance of the lack of "having" from the rivalry between the sexes is unmistakable. She counts the men with whom she goes out, calming herself at seeing that she really has one. If one is missing, she is deeply depressed.

In Ophelia's compulsion, the body-object searched for is an erogenous object and at the same time an object of need.

Behind that impossible-seeming body of love hides another body: that of the child she fears she will never have. "To give oneself a child" can be a variant of "to give oneself a body". The despair of wanting a man hides another despair, in which biology lets its cry be heard in the danger that stalks her of remaining forever excluded from the physical experience of maternity, which lends itself to the phantasy of the greatest carnal fusion.

Ophelia begs the "other" to nourish her narcissistically and to free her from the suffering caused by the lack of trophic narcissism with his presence and his "body to body". She begs him thus to occupy alternately the place of "two" (in the reconstruction of the dyad with the primal maternal object) and the place of "three" (call for the father, for triangulation). When this attempt at structuralization fails, Ophelia sees herself sent back to a shattered unity, to a solitude intolerable in that it is not propped up by the presence of a sufficiently good internal object.

Her compulsion to "another body" leaves bare her feeling of despair, which is anchored in a melancholic oral fixation (Bodni, 1991) that manifests itself in the repetitive compulsion to failure and pathological mourning.

CHAPTER THREE

Feminine orgasms

Introduction

I know that my position is controversial and differs from conventional ideas about the way a woman approaches pleasure and enjoyment.

I want to emphasize that we are talking about "feminine" orgasms and not women's orgasms; I want to insist on a space that is properly feminine, which, because of the bisexuality inborn in every human subject, can have its effect on a man or a woman. And yet, in accordance with the famous phrase "anatomy is fate", it is the woman who has an easy path to the voluptuousness with which I shall occupy myself in the following pages.

The male finds in his visible penis the physical place, narcissistically invested, in which to concentrate his libido. This penis must, in addition, carry out a perceptible and tangible process of erection, friction, and ejaculation, which gives direction to his sexual activity in all erogenous encounters.

The woman lacks this visible organ, which has given so much to talk about in psychoanalysis. Her lack of a penis will be a source of early anxieties, referred to by pioneers contemporary with Freud (Horney, 1933; Jones, 1927; Klein, 1975), partly derived from the fact that her very anatomy prevents the little girl from perceiving the indemnity of her genitals in the context of the events of her phantasy world and the effects of masturbation (the girl's disadvantage, Melanie Klein says). Her sexual organs are located within the body and cannot be seen, nor controlled.

Nevertheless, as I understand it, it is that same anatomy that facilitates the diffusion of eroticism over the surface of her whole body, and thus the possibility of erogenous zones that expand, contract and grow.

From this point of view not to have a penis is an advantage for the woman. It is not for nothing that legend puts into the mouth of Tiresias the idea that she has more enjoyment than man—ten times more, seven times more, say the different versions. In the comparison of enjoyment made by Tiresias (who lived transformed into a woman for seven years), it is the femininity of the woman that can give her an inexhaustible wealth of orgasms.

Psychoanalysis has not taken much notice of orgasms. The dominance of sexologists was largely responsible for this. Freud only refers to orgasm about a dozen times and always tangentially—possibly because he sees it as something intermediate between body and mind.

I consider that feminine orgasm is something subversive. It challenges the laws of biology by the diversity of manifestations it involves. In the Tiresias legend, it is interesting to recall the goddess Hera's anger when Tiresias proves his knowledge of the extent of enjoyment in women. The erogenous wealth of woman ought to be secret, hidden; I might almost add that there is a hint of "elitism" in the sense that it is reserved for women, not for all.

It becomes essential at this point to free the concept of erogenous zone from the anatomical precision with which it was designated at the dawn of psychoanalysis and give it a wider sense, in which we can find it logical to talk about something that can narcissize any part of the body, any area of skin, any orifice. As already established, Freud (1926d [1925]) introduces the idea of an ego-function of an organ attached to its erogeneity. This erogeneity closely depends on the sexual signification that an organ acquires at a given moment. As I have already said, the body is like a Moebius strip that demonstrates the continuity between outside and inside, between its surface and its internal parts.

The human body negates the laws of biology when it starts an erogenous affective sensorial interchange with another body. It can then reveal how it has passed beyond the language of which it has been the object, and it leads us astray by unfolding a multiplicity of intimate changes. The different combinations of phenomena show the intersections between perceptions and sensations, between words and gestures, phantasies and erogenous emanations, memories and inhibitions.

The body in its feminine aspect brings out its own ghosts. It is a "different" body, in which the essence of its erogenous expression plays its part in a tantalizingly hidden terrain. This feminine condition creates mystery and . . . incomprehension.

Having arrived at a world that the imagination sees as "not having" (a penis), it is the woman, nevertheless, who has to play the main part in the fundamental adventures of the body: menstruation, pregnancy, childbirth, breast-feeding . . . orgasms. Like the blood in menstruation, milk in lactation, the baby in childbirth, orgasm also has to emerge from the body like one more change in her enigmatic sensuality.

All attempts to circumscribe the feminine orgasm will result in an incomplete view—sometimes even a ridiculous one—which will attempt to apply a single model of sexual satisfaction, tending to obstruct the revelation of the feminine enigma.

The usual psychoanalytic definition of the feminine orgasm is paradoxical. On the one hand, it is seen as purely biological, while at the same time as something independent, something that can be easily defined at one moment but defies categorization at the next.

Feminine orgasms are not exact or measurable. They are erratic, changing, elusive. They unfold in a field with no exigencies, where anything goes, free from any demands that they keep to a precise form.

Before developing my ideas in more detail, I believe it may be useful to look at a little history—to go back to consider how Freud saw women in the early years of the discovery of psychoanalysis.

Freud and feminine sexuality (1895–1905)

First, I shall consider the text "On the Grounds for Detaching a Particular Syndrome from Neurasthenia under the Description 'Anxiety Neurosis'" (1895b [1894]) and "Draft G" (in 1950 [1892–1899]). In the first, Freud already states the problem posed by the confused and artificial oscillations of the feminine sexual instinct, and, undertaking to compare the man's sexuality with that of the woman, he writes:

> In women too we must postulate a somatic sexual excitation and a state in which this excitation becomes a psychical stimulus—libido—and provokes the urge to the specific action to which voluptuous feeling is attached. Where women are concerned, however, we are not in a position to say what the process analogous to the relaxation of tension of the seminal vesicles may be. [1895b [1894], p. 109]

We can see that Freud has clearly perceived that, as far as feminine sensuality is concerned, masculine linearity is blurred and gives way to oscillations, to new forms that escape the classical model represented by male sexuality. In the same way we see a Freud who persists in discovering exact anatomo-physiological correspondences between one manner of sexual functioning and another, and who fails on both occasions, showing how this epistemological obstacle raises itself as a barrier on the road to knowledge.

"Draft G" includes the "schema of sexuality", which is enormously rich for the study of feminine sensuality. It is practically devoted to woman; there he enumerates his hypotheses about sexual anaesthesia and woman's melancholy. I want to reproduce the schema, in order to indicate a few important elements (Figure 1). In principle it is a question of four quadrants, dividing horizontally the soma from the psyche, and vertically the internal world from the external world. On the internal side he includes the terminal organ, the source of sexual excitation, the rachidian centre as well as numerous roads leading to and from the psychic sexual group located in the super-external quadrant. The roads transport sexual tension and voluptuous feelings. One of the most interesting aspects of the schema lies in the interaction with the external

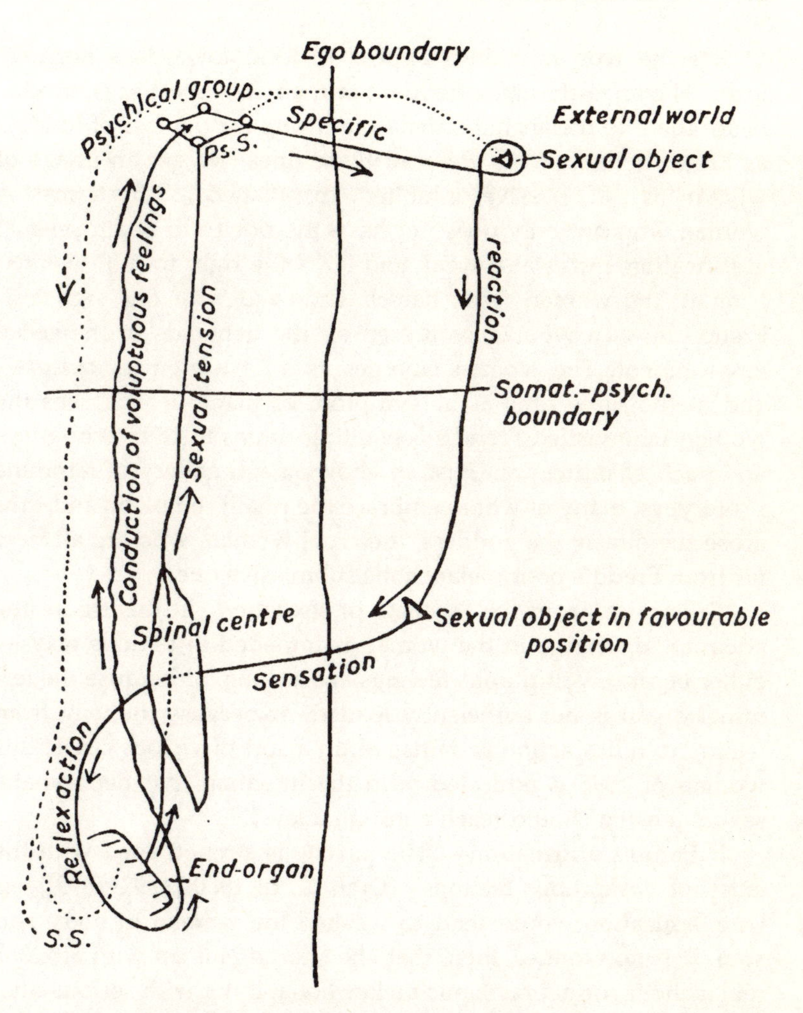

FIGURE 1 *Schematic picture of sexuality*

world—that is, when, passing the limit of the ego, the specific action takes place in search of the sexual object, which is found in the external world. The intention of this movement is to approach the sexual object to the point of making it step over the psychosomatic limit and putting it in a favourable position. The erogenous bodies come into contact, feeling emerges, and discharge approaches.

For the woman, things appear to tend towards a negative form. The anaesthesia so frequent in them, as Freud says, predisposes them to melancholy, that "mourning for the loss of libido", as Freud defines it. As we read these lines, we get an image of woman as sad, passive, inhibited, dissatisfied ... hysterical. A woman who not only does not have the power to attain sensual gratification, but is also weak and lacks the right to it. Prevented from it, the woman finds herself endowed with one sign less. Freud shows a woman paralysed by the demands of the social environment. The woman emerges as a "symptom of culture", and at the same time as a "symptom of man". It describes the women who visited Freud's consulting-rooms in 1895, who mark an epoch of repression. History shows a full gallery of feminine prototypes, many of whom embrace the phallic emblem, and thus arose the queen, the goddess, the cruel woman, who are all very far from Freud's poor melancholic submissive one.

Taking up again the "schema of sexuality", in this figure the adequate discharge in the woman is impeded in various ways—either because voluptuous feelings are lacking, or because the terminal organ is not sufficiently loaded, or because the way from feeling to reflex action is damaged. In a sort of vicious circle, this woman of 1895 is educated with the intention that her somatic sexual tension should reach a minimal level.

If Freud's affirmation—"The psyche is strengthened with the entry of voluptuous feelings" (Draft G, in 1950 [1892–1899])—is true, education would tend to weaken the woman in body and soul. It is no wonder, then, that she should end up with anxious melancholia, or neurasthenic melancholia, if not with serious melancholia.

I quote a paragraph: "The question has to be considered of how it comes about that anaesthesia is so predominant a characteristic of women. It arises from the passive part played by them. An anaesthetic man will soon cease to undertake any coitus; a woman has no choice" (1950 [1892–1899], p. 204). Freud goes on to give the main reasons for her propensity towards anaesthesia. The first has already been mentioned: education demands "that she give up resource to specific reaction [see Figure 1] and that she should adopt instead permanent specific actions, destined to induce the specific action in the masculine individual". The dotted road that goes from the sex-object to the psychic sex-group thus indicates the circuit in which a feminine position must be maintained by constantly stimulating the object, but located in the famous decoy tactic of coquetry and seductive snares. Freud considers that this movement of inhibiting reaction in the woman is necessary (hence the importance of educating her with the least possible somatic sexual tension), since if, on the contrary "the somatic sexual tension were reinforced, the psychic sexual group would not delay in acquiring intermittently a power such that, as happens in men, it would put the sex-object in a favourable position by means of a specific reaction". Education, then, must mark the difference, if not of the sexes, of the attitudes of conquest and appropriation of the sex-object. According to Assoun (1983), "the woman would be condemned to function in a way that is at once deficient in the line of objectivity and over-demanding in the line of the Other" (p. 103). Undoubtedly in the light of these reflections, the woman-system establishes a functional antagonism.

But even when this instinctual arrangement is organized in a female human subject, it is not the end of the affair. The terms in which Freud refers to her make this clear: "enigmatic", "incomprehensible", "insincere". The "without" or "not having" that describe her anatomy are transformed to not having words to define her erogenous world, being "without" an exact place in which precisely to locate the source of her pleasure.

One is far from thinking of a feminine capacity for erogenous metamorphosis or of a potentiality for expansion of her desiring flesh that is alien to the known canons. Precisely—as we shall see in the following vignettes of Freud—when a woman enters into intense enjoyment it is masked by hysteria. Anaesthesia is considered as a lesser evil compared with the feminine loss of self-control (see Letter 102 of the Freud–Fliess correspondence, in 1950 [1892–1899]), which the science of psychoanalysis does not seem to understand.

In his eagerness to compare feminine sexuality with masculine, Freud uses terms that, when applied to a woman's body, attract attention today: erection, pollution. Not only does he lack appropriate terms to define feminine sensual events, he also insists on a parallel between the man's sexual functioning and that of the woman. He does not perceive the infinity of shades, leaps, and suspensions of feminine eroticism.

In addition to using the terms "erection" and "pollution", Freud begins to emphasize the sensation of urinating in the field of female excitability. In his work on "The Neuro-Psychoses of Defence" (1894a) he tells of the case of a girl who was afraid of being attacked by urinary incontinence—a phobia that incapacitated her for social life. He discovered that this desire had arisen for the first time in a concert hall where she was seated next to a gentleman to whom she was not indifferent. He goes on:

> She began to think about him and imagine herself sitting beside him as his wife. During this erotic reverie she had the bodily sensation which is to be compared with erection in a man and which in her case—I do not know whether this is always so—ended with a slight need to urinate . . . The erection was each time accompanied by the need to urinate, though without making any impression on her until the scene in the concert hall. The treatment led to an almost complete control over the phobia. [Freud, 1894a, p. 178]

The term "erection" was given a definite place in the woman's body. *Terms from a different anatomy imposed themselves on her anatomy.* It was too revolutionary in those times for psychoanalytic thought to give a specific terminology to erogenous phenomena that were incomprehensible and caused astonishment, if not irritability. Probably—I have to repeat this idea various times throughout this book—a quota of mystery is inherent in femininity, and this requires a certain amount of inexplicability and ignorance—as though there were repeated in this ignorance something of the original uncertainty in the face of a magical aspect of the feminine, that which is rooted in another essential ignorance, which has to do with being in the world—an ignorance that religions appease but which subsists in the most secret parts of the human soul.

Returning to the case described, the novelty of the importance it attributes to the sensations of urinating in the woman is what brings out the erogenous power of all that lies between a woman's legs, not limiting it to the clitoris as the only generator of pleasant sensations. He even adds: "this young woman, whom all sexual reality horrified, not even conceiving that she might marry one day, was, on the other hand, of such sexual hyperaesthesia that in the erotic phantasies to which she gladly abandoned herself she regularly experienced the voluptuous sense referred to."

This case also helped me to realize the dissociation of erotic life in the woman. Freud (1910a) dealt with this theme when referring to the sexuality of man: tenderness with the mother–spouse and eroticism with the prostitute. In women, dissociation takes place in the following way: respect, tenderness, and modesty with the gentleman and eroticism in phantasies. *The woman's brothel was her phantasy.* There, in secret, she could give free rein to her libido and experience voluptuous sensations beyond measure.

Still in 1895, "Draft J" confirms for us the direction of Freud's ideas at that period. The lower abdomen as the seat of voluptuous sensations is explored again. Mrs. PJ has been married for three months. Her husband has had to go away, she misses him, and to distract herself she sings and plays the piano. Suddenly "she felt ill—in her abdomen and stomach, her head swam, she had feelings of oppression and anxiety and cardiac paraesthesia; she thought she was going mad. A moment later it occurred to her that she had eaten eggs and mushrooms that morning, and concluded she had been poisoned. However, the condition quickly passed off". Freud (Draft J, in 1950 [1892–1899]) states with the confidence of genius: "She had had a longing for her husband, that is for sexual relations with him. She had thus come upon an idea which had excited sexual effect, and afterwards defence against the idea; she had then taken fright and made a false connection or substitution" (p. 216).

He uses a very graphic word—*Liebeserguss*[1]—which can be translated as outpouring or overflow of love. Mrs. PJ would have taken fright at the danger of losing control, of letting herself go and finding herself with the hyperaesthesia at the other side of frigidity. She then reinterprets her perceptions from a pathological angle (poisoned by mushrooms) in which paranoia appears.

Interested by the urethral erogenization that he has investigated in woman and using pressure on the forehead, Freud extracts a double confession from his patient: in the first place that she had a longing for conjugal sexual caresses, and in the second place that she experienced "a sensation in the lower abdomen, a convulsive desire to urinate". Freud suggests urethral erogenous sensations, which she confirms. But Freud is not satisfied, even when he has managed to localize the source of pleasure. The unnameable element persists and prompts Freud to say: ". . . The insincerity of women starts from their omitting the characteristic sexual symptoms in describing their states. So it had really been an *orgasm*" [Freud's word in German was *"Pollution"*] (1950 [1892–1899], p. 217). Once again he uses a term taken from masculine sexuality.

How can it be thought, Mrs. PJ, that that overflowing sensation that suddenly breaks in, that convulsive longing to urinate, that emotional wave (pleasure–unpleasure), comes from a body of desire? Without a manifest object, without a locatable source, without a quantifiable and known ending? Strange manifestations, in any case, when a woman begins to unveil the mysteries of her sensuality, from ignorance of the untransmittable, from experience of what is not spoken about, of which little is known—perhaps the convulsive desire to urinate, which, Freud supposes, is no more than the expression of instinctual force tending towards discharge, and here too urinating may be an attempt to give orgasm a locatable organic label—a convulsive desire to enjoy, through the bladder, through the abdomen, through any place.

It would appear that the lack of "characteristic sexual symptoms" irritates Freud when in reality it constitutes an intrinsic element of the feminine being. Mrs PJ's convulsive desire might have sought different erogenous zones to manifest itself.

I want to cite one last quotation from Freud which dates from the same period. This is the final paragraph of Letter 102 to Fliess (18th January 1899, in 1950 [1892–1899]). He says:

> Of a third woman I have had this most interesting information. An important and wealthy man (bank director), aged about 60, came to see me and entertained me with the peculiarities of a girl with whom he has a liaison. I threw out a guess that she was probably quite anaesthetic. On the contrary she has from four to six orgasms [*Entladungen:* discharges] during one coitus. But at the very first approach she is seized with a tremor, and immediately afterwards falls into a pathological sleep, during which she talks as though she were in hypnosis,

> carries out post-hypnotic suggestions and has complete amnesia for the whole condition. He is going to marry her off, and she will certainly be anaesthetic with her husband. The old gentleman, through the possibility of being identified with the immensely powerful father of her childhood, evidently has the effect of being able to set free the libido attached to her phantasies. Instructive! [p. 89]

Feminine erogeneity fluctuates between anaesthesia and hyperaesthesia, both considered pathological. An aroma of the "rare, mysterious" overflows from these women's bodies filled with their voluptuousness. My attention is also drawn, in this last case, to the condemnation to frigidity once she is married, of which Freud speaks as though it were very far from his thinking that to have many orgasms could be a possibility in the erotic life of a woman. In his thought she remains limited to giving free rein to her voluptuous dreams, as he himself expresses it, in phantasies or in semi-hypnotic trances in which she brings out her organic repressions.

* * *

Throughout his work Freud failed to find the parallel between feminine and masculine sexuality. Then he asked: What does a woman want, what does she desire?—and he coined the suggestive image of the "dark continent" (1926e).

I leave here my reflections on Freud's ideas on femininity. I cannot fail to mention how, almost at the end of his life, writing his last works on feminine sexuality (1933a) in his brilliance and his anxiety for deeper investigation on this theme, he wrote that beautiful phrase in which he asked for help from everyone's experience of life, poets and women themselves, to explain to him the keys of a sexuality which left him perplexed and the solution to which he left unfinished.

The primal orgasm and the process of orgasmization

Freud (1905d) describes the effects of the pleasant sucking of a baby as "a sort of orgasm". A little further on he writes:

> No one who has seen a baby sinking back satiated from the breast and falling asleep with flushed cheeks and a blissful smile can escape the reflection that this picture persists as a prototype of the expression of sexual satisfaction in later life. [p. 182]

This sort of orgasm relaxes the whole body and makes one sleepy. In an earlier work (Alizade, 1989) I called it "primal orgasm" —as a predecessor of the erogenous climaxes that will take place later in the course of the subject's erotic life. This primal orgasm shows its condition of expansion over the surface of the body before the establishment of the sexual difference and of all notion of conflict. It reveals the incestuous, inbreeding link that will later lie behind every erotic bond. The joyful mouth–breast relationship (Freud, 1905d, 1916–17) awakens similarly the first erogenous genital tingles during sucking.

Starting from this orgasm-precursor of suckling, specific psycho-somatic movements appear as the love-life takes its particular course in each individual.

The primal orgasm belongs to both men and women. It takes place on the body of the primal object, that *preferred form* configured by the maternal body, a woman's body, rounded and warm, a form that "gives" and "nourishes". As a reward for the pleasant work of feeding itself, the infant receives beatific satisfaction after suckling, by which it is wrapped and supported. The instincts of self-preservation and sex function in unison. Sensuality is naturally stimulated. The small body surface of the suckling allows maximum contact between all its skin, all the surface of its body with that of the mother who feeds it. The preliminary pleasure plays a basic role in this "erotic life of the suckling", which is full of sensations, perceptions, and sensual discharges.

In the primal orgasm during lactation, three components enter into play which affect the incipient erogenous links: the orificial or deep component, the epidermic or surface component, and the component in which the interior of the body is involved. The orificial component includes the breast with the nipple through which the milk flows into the mouth of the infant. The epidermic and sensorial surface component includes the enormous variety of sti-muli that comprise the skin of the infant and the world of its senses (sights, touches, muscular pressures, rubbing of skin, odours . . .). The third component introduces the interior of the body and the sensation of satiety or repletion. Didier Anzieu stresses (1985) that "If the mouth provides the first experience, lively and short, of a distinguishing contact, of a place of passage or of incorporation, repletion gives the suckling the more diffuse, more durable, experience of a central mass, a fullness, a centre of gravity" (p. 35).

The primal orgasm, including these experiences of plenitude in the frame of an affective-nourishing interchange, can be considered as a primitive organizer of the feeling of balance, of the constitution of the skin-ego (D. Anzieu, 1985) or of the nucleus of stone, which I described earlier.

The primal orgasm constitutes a *principal* envelope, an invisible protective wall against the displeasure that would permit a return to the first moments of existence (intrauterine life) and a recovery of the integrity of the senses in the service of the principle of Nirvana.

It plays a very important part as an unconscious physical memory in feminine sensuality. Suckling after suckling, voluptuousness after voluptuousness, satiety in short, is, at the same time an indicator of erogenous satiety. The biological requirement of feeding and that of desire are conjoined to produce this first enjoyment for which both instincts (those of self-preservation and sex) work together.

The primal orgasm shows its state of expansion over the body surface before the establishment of the sex difference and before any notion of conflict. It reveals the incestuous, inbreeding link that will later pulsate behind every erotic bond. It constitutes the first outline of the synthesis of the senses in an integrating perceptive sensorial–affective acme.

The primal orgasm is founded upon a form of pre-linguistic pleasure.

It is an early erogenous–affective experience, which influences the illusory unconscious projects of recovering the first dyad. This has acquired the status of an idyllic representation of complete bliss without any demands in the service of primary narcissism and the pleasure principle. It is an imaginary illusion that is destroyed by the reality principle but persists as a backdrop in the erotic life of every individual.

The "schema of sexuality" (Freud, 1950 [1892–1899]), mentioned above, as well as some sections of the "Project" (1950 [1895]) are very useful for observing in detail successive orders of sensual phenomena interacting in the instinctual and desiring body, namely somatic sexual tension, psychic sexual tension, voluptuous sensations, experiences of satisfaction, experiences of pain, experiences of pleasure. The putting into action of this affective–erogenous psychic machinery prefigures the "primal erogenous matrix" in which are recorded the first experiences of pleasure and/or suffering that take place in the interchange with the first love-objects. These erogenous and affective experiences depict alternating polarities of love–hate, attraction–rejection, pain–satisfaction. With time, successive changes of meaning take place as the complementary series exert their effects upon it. On the substratum of the primal erogenous matrix changing figures are traced during the course of different experiences. Rhythms, temperatures, movements, internal organs will become sources of libido (Freud, 1905d). This map will be composed of erogenous zones, facilitated or perhaps easily erogenizable, others mute, others intermediate, and of specific stimuli that will trigger or inhibit excitement, sensation, affect.

The words of significant others make their marks on that body, which, first desired, conforms and becomes desirous in its turn. The word thus outlines erogenous zones and fixes spaces that are now narcissistically valued, now underestimated. In addition, words carry the weight of the somatic support of whoever speaks them, and in that interchange bodies act secretly and are doubly marked: in the register of representation and in that of affect.

The "process of organization" meets its first linking point in the erogenous matrix. That oral body that licks, sucks, kisses, sucks in, and incorporates imprints on the psyche the first stammering traces of an interchange of desire. It is a first honeymoon that the paths of libido are leaving behind.

I want to bring out the supreme importance of this erogenous matrix and of the traces in the unconscious memory and the primal orgasms as regards feminine sensuality. These first links are installed in the dimension "before words". The repetition of these pleasant experiences leaves established the base on which, in successive psycho-corporeal apprenticeships, are formed new memory-traces of erogenous perceptions and of waves of voluptuousness. On this primitive sensuality there will accumulate the different phases (oral, anal, phallic) that will distinguish in this way the principal erogenous zones (mouth, anus, clitoris, vagina).

The primal orgasm is a first form of enjoyment, with the participation of the death instinct fused with the life instinct. The world of feminine orgasms, in its richness and variety, is rooted in this primal matrix, where the primal orgasm has its home. Feminine voluptuousness owes much to it.

Three touching movements

I want to specify three configurations of touching that alternate with the times of life. Their sequence is chronological on the one hand, and on the other hand these configurations alternate in the course of experiences and instinctual conflicts. I shall name them: "whole body", "do not touch" and "touch again".

Whole body

This is the time of the infant when everything that can be done with the baby's body is permitted, even recommended. The more it is touched, caressed, or manipulated, the better. The Hindus massage their babies beautifully; the Eskimos carry them naked, clinging to their mothers' shoulders. The body-to-body attempts to reach the highest possible degree of contact. According to Didier Anzieu (1985), this constant skin-to-skin contact in the Eskimos guarantees the individual's tranquil tolerance of the inclemencies of life—that is, it accounts for the strong and tranquil Eskimo stock. In the realm of the primary process and of psychic immaturity, to touch all the surface of the infant constitutes an act of protection, of health. The "whole body"—that nourishing–affective intimate interchange at the stage before words—is a time of interaction of presences (flesh against flesh, sense with sense, archaisms of the infant with archaisms of the mother). To be, to feel, to touch, to interchange are appropriate verbs to describe this deep, intense moment in which the stimulation of the senses and the bodily functions begins and in which the other (the mother) leads the infantile subject to the recognition of its body through the contribution of her own body, with its material dimension and in its somato-psychic achievements. When it moves across the mother's body, the first body of care poured over it—so to speak—which initiates it into emotional interaction, the baby organizes sensations, registers both positive and negative experiences that will later acquire new meanings, and arms its record with a particular, unique *senti* (D. Anzieu, 1970).

The "whole body" is affected by the smallness of the body surface of the recently born baby in comparison with that of the adult subject, which easily leads to an almost complete touching that embraces the epidermic surface and the orifices subjected to it (rectum, mouth, ears, genitals). Similarly, there is innocent contact, without disgust, with the secretions (faeces, urine etc.). Organic repression (Freud, 1930a) does not exist between mother and child, and tranquil intimacy finds its form of maximum expression.

The body of the infant is stripped naked, looked at, oiled, kissed by those others who are important to it. It is moved, measured, dandled. Instinctual gratification is directed to the satisfaction of the instinct of self-preservation in suckling and the sex-instinct through the mother's caresses. On the other hand, half-inhibited instincts are expressed in tenderness. Naturally, the death instinct and the instinct of power also act on the new-born.

Do not touch

On the basis of the structural prohibition of incest and parricide (Freud, *Totem and Taboo,* 1912–13), touching has its limits. Seduction and castration are elements that intervene at this moment. The trophic touching of the "whole body" will gradually come up against various barriers. Tenderness has turned to seduction, and the desire for incest will have to be symbolized and displaced into the metaphorical and metonymic chain. Bodies separate, and the erogenous zones are distinguished. The "whole body" gives place to a body with clearly distinguished parts. The body remains alone in its entry into the world of civilization. The castration phantasy sets up barriers of prohibition. Erogenous contacts are becoming subject to laws, and the permissiveness of the baby is left behind. Now organic repressions are being established; one does not touch one's own faeces; disgust and shame emerge as sexual barriers, while a succession of erogenous sensations attached to phantasies are outlined within the frame of everything that is prohibited. This prohibition is necessary. Didier Anzieu (1985, ch. 10) points out that the prohibition to touch concerns equally the two basic instincts of self-preservation and sex. He writes: "Do not touch inanimate objects which could break or could hurt you; do not exert excessive force on parts of the body of other people. . . . Do not persistently touch your body or other people's bodies, in areas sensitive to pleasure, or you will find yourself overwhelmed by an excitement that you are incapable of understanding or satisfying. (This prohibition is precisely to protect the child from sexuality, both its own and that of others.) In both cases prohibiting touching guards against excessive excitation and its consequence, the overflowing of impulse." Further on, he specifies: "The prohibition to touch separates the region of the familiar, the region protected and protecting, from the alien region, disquieting and dangerous."

The interior is distinguished from the exterior, and spaces are created. The infant *is* dressed. The prohibition of touching applies both to objects (do not touch electric plugs, fire, etc.) and to its own body in its erogenous character (do not touch your genitals). The parents' bodies also are covered with a veil of modesty.[2]

Primal innocence has disappeared. Maturity has come, with its quota of sacrifice and suffering. The reality principle marks the road to frustration, and the inaccessibility of desire is entangled with the knots that conflicts generate in the psyche.

In transgressing the prohibition, the overcoming of this limit and the dimension of the discovery will come into play. The plasticity of prohibition allows it to be transgressed at times in honour of a successful sublimation and to be established again without disturbing of the internal equilibrium. The authority rooted in prohibition and maintained by the superego will be sufficiently good to give place to the movement of transgression. Freud (1910c), in his work on Leonardo da Vinci, considers this important point and outlines the concept of transgression in his idea of escaping the intimidation exerted by the father-figure. This possibility of escape frees the individual from internal coercions and opens to him the narrow field of the new, of that which is to come. Freud writes: "In most other human beings—no less today than in primaeval times—the need for support from an authority of some sort is so compelling that their world begins to totter if that authority is threatened." Only Leonardo could dispense with that support; he would not have been able to do so had he not learnt in the first years of his life to do without his father. His later scientific research, with all its boldness and independence, presupposed the existence of infantile sexual researches uninhibited by his father, and was a prolongation of them with the sexual element excluded.

> When anyone has, like Leonardo, escaped being intimidated by his father during his earliest childhood, and has in his researches cast away the fetters of authority, it would be in the sharpest contradiction to our expectation if we found that he had remained a believer and had been unable to escape from dogmatic religion. [1910c, pp. 122–123]

I deal with this aspect of prohibition here because although feminine sensuality may appear to move in a terrain very far from sublimation and transgression, it is important to note that transgression occurs basically in erotic experience and in mystic experience that is similar to it, and that, in addition, every amorous bond brings into play this dimension of sublimation in which even in the greatest sensorial–erogenous interchange an area is reserved for the non-sexual, for the desexualized impulse that is externalized in the sublime element of the link, in mutual admiration, respect, and exalted contemplation.

So to consider the prohibition of touching leads into the territories of obedience and disobedience. The prohibition of touching is succeeded by the third movement of touching, which I will describe now.

Touching again

This section gives the history of the entire love-life of a subject and the bodies whom he will touch with his eroticism, his tenderness, his affect, his imagination. In the midst of the order established by prohibition, the coming into play of the interchanges of desire causes a return to chaos, to the primal instinctuality. With a normal background of inhibition, but given an unconscious knowledge of the primal experiences before words, multiple resonances would influence the directions that eroticism has to take in each subject. And as the prohibition to touch isolates the subject in a certain way, inviting him to mark out a space for himself, touching again invites submersion in another body, or in his own. Touching one another leads to a rediscovery of bodily interchanges that happened either with the metamorphosis of puberty or with the passing of time. This recognition of an erogenous body in oneself disturbs the psychic economy of the individual faced with the urge towards discharge, towards the search for the object, towards the blossoming of phantasies in masturbation. If the first movement of "whole body" is basically a passive time of being touched, this third period inaugurates the changes of "going towards", of putting into effect the specific action, either by taking the initiative or by functioning at the level of the lure, magically attracting the object of desire.

The exploration of the other body brings into the foreground the theme—already approached—of transgression in the dialectic relationship, which it maintains through prohibition. Touching again implies exploring the world, touching it with the body and with the mind, touching it with emotion; it implies coming into the open.

The erogenous body is like another body lying in wait, which catches fire with every contact, with every bodily coupling, in which marks on the skin let us see traits of yesterday in facilitations and obstacles. Each time will be a repetition and a recommencement. The identifying process allows different personages to hide under the same body and emerge at different moments.

Touching again is moving at the same time towards the new and towards what was first known (the mother's body). On the chosen body, therefore, incest and parricide always intervene, limiting erogenous emanations and causing explosions and overflows. Starting from here, we can conjecture at one moment about the basic unfaithfulness of the flesh (in the same body live many beings, which phantasy awakens and convokes) and at another moment about an inevitable faithfulness to the primal object.

The path of femininity and its relationship with orgasm

In feminine sensuality the primal erogenization established with the first interchange between mother and new-born child is fundamental. According to Aulagnier (1975), there occurs "a double meeting, with the body and with the productions of the mother's psyche". In this dyad, the "primal violence" exercised by the desiring mother is imposed on the incipient bodily ego of the newly born. This desire of the mother on the body of the infant is the first penetration that the flesh receives as it becomes really human—that is, a speaking being. The interaction of two mutually desiring bodies creates a field of maximum intimacy. Erogenization extends beyond the erogenous zones in caresses, looks, and the bath of words that floods the newly born. The "primal orgasm" takes place—oral orgasm, in accordance with the source of the instinct, or orgasm of the whole body if we believe in the diffusion of eroticism throughout the baby's body. Once again I want to refer to the first body-to-body in which a first sketch of the "between-women" dimension appears between the mother and the little girl. The woman's body occupies the place of "preferred form" in that it constitutes the primal body on which the first fundamental experiences are formed. The initial desirous interchange for every feminine subject takes place in this "homosensual" territory, which gives rise to the first structurizing speculation.

Oral eroticism is early transferred to the penis, following the penis–breast equation (Jones, 1927; Klein, 1975). Freud (1910c) also mentions this equivalence in his work on Leonardo da Vinci:

> The inclination to take a man's sexual organ into the mouth and suck at it, which in respectable society is considered a loathsome sexual perversion, is nevertheless found with great frequency among women of today . . . and in the state of being in love it appears completely to lose its repulsive character . . .; this situation, which morality condemns with such severity, may be traced to an origin of the most innocent kind. It only repeats in a different form a situation in which we all once felt comfortable—when we were still in our suckling days . . . and took our mother's (or wet-nurse's) nipple into our mouth and sucked at it. The organic impression of this experience—the first source of pleasure in our life—doubtless remains indelibly printed on us. [p. 86]

This leads me to think that the first deflowering of the infant *is* constituted by lactation (the mother's breast penetrates into the mouth of the infant). If the penis–breast equation is successfully achieved, penetration will be easier in youth, when in phantasy the similarity is felt between opening the mouth to receive the swollen breast from which flows nourishing milk—as happened yesterday—and today's opening of the legs to receive the tender penis, deprived of violence and humiliation.

The early erogenous idylls are interrupted due to the conflict generated in the little girl by the difference of the sexes. The penis, with its narcissistic charge, appears in its libidinal evolution. And even when the vagina, a virtual space, is the seat of early sensations, this does not prevent the greatest value being set on the penis, the ideal image of an organ, a sex. A sort of "biological tragedy" seems to mark her sexual being with no penis. She has not got one, or has lost it, or "it will grow some time", she thinks, and all these are mortifying options. "Castrated", she will envy the idealized object whose possession would calm her anxiety. The phallic value is still ascribed to the penis and its metaphorical–metonymic displacements. From the bond with the anatomical origins, everything masculine usually appears as a fetish, contaminated by that impossible power attributed to the phallus.

Phallocentric culture impedes to a certain extent the good outcome of the woman's erogenous path, intensifying the little girl's natural envy of the man's genitals and facilitating her alienation in an ideal of sexuality that moves her away from femininity.

In other cultures this does not happen in the same way. I quote a fragment by Margaret Mead (1946), which seems to me beautifully illustrative:

> In Bali, little girls between two and three walk much of the time with purposely thrust out little bellies, and the older women tap them playfully as they pass. 'Pregnant,' they tease. So the little girl learns that although the signs of her membership in her own sex are slight, her breasts mere tiny buttons no bigger then her brother's, her genitals a simple inconspicuous fold, some day she will be pregnant, some day she will have a baby. And having a baby is, on the whole, one of the most exciting and conspicuous achievements that can be presented to the eyes of small children in these simple worlds . . . Furthermore, the little girl learns that she will have a baby not because she is strong or energetic or initiating, not because she works and struggles and tries, and in the end succeeds, but simply because she is a girl and not a boy, and girls turn into women, and in the end—if they protect their femininity—have babies. [p. 97]

Undoubtedly, a certain trophic hate, a certain distance, must arise if the mother is to be abandoned as love-object and the father take her place. This hate may need to reach very high levels when the pre-oedipal bond has been very intense and full of conflicts. With regard to those cases, Freud writes:

> The women patients showing a strong attachment to their mother in whom I have been able to study the pre-Oedipus past have all told me that when their mother gave them enemas or rectal douches they used to offer the greatest resistance and react with fear and screams of rage . . . compare the outbreak of anger after an enema to the orgasm following genital excitation. [1931b, pp. 237–238]

At the appearance of an orgasmic equivalent (fury), the phantasy of the phallic mother emerges. The enema, penetrating the little girl's anus, reactivates the frustrations and satisfactions of which the mother-object was the support. In this scenario a drama of needs develops, and the deep wound of infantile narcissism makes its presence felt.

If she wants to become a woman, she will have to accept that one day she will receive a penis in the form of a child, and she must be happy to accept male authority. This is what Freud says; otherwise the destiny of woman has, according to him, three possible paths: the complex of masculinity, renouncing of all sexuality, and homosexual object-choice.

I want to mention a paragraph by Dolto (1982) that is particularly relevant to the genitalization of women. She writes:

> In order that desire may appear in the woman's genital zone, in accordance with the functional needs of the penis, that is to say in order that it may be penetrable, it is necessary that her girl-nature should have been well received by her parents at her birth, and that the oral period of her childhood, including weaning, should have run a normal course; if it has remained negative or defensive towards the mother's partially phallic object (the breast) she would run the risk of inflicting on the man the mutilation of the penis during coitus due to the oral cathexis of the vagina. It is also necessary that her vagina should have been valued in the period of mourning for the magical anal child which she supposed babies to be for women, in order to resist the danger of violation which she might suffer due to the cathexis of her vagina, which, like an anus, would be inhabited by centrifugal phallic dynamics in relation to the partial object. *It is even necessary that desire in the woman should be indifferent as far as her vagina is concerned, that she should not have invested it absolutely, either actively or passively,* that she should simply ignore it, or that it should be the sort of attraction towards a centripetal penis, more powerful than the destructive options which could inhabit it. [p. 290]

The italics in these lines are mine. I want to emphasize this "neutral" state of the vagina to which Dolto alludes and which has to do with the "minimum demand" to which I refer later on as a facilitating condition of vaginal orgasm.

Deviating from Freud, I propose (see chapter seven) a conclusion about the Oedipus complex in the woman. Beyond the acceptance of castration another space opens, the territory of the feminine properly speaking. Alienated in the pointless levelling of sexual difference, this ambit was ignored and has to be found in the transit to femininity. In the space of analytical transference, transmission also takes place, and this, too, is favourable to the attainment of the gradual revealing of this dormant virtuality.

Goldstein (1983) writes:

> It has been a very deep-rooted prejudice in psychoanalysis to consider—with Freud—the girl's psychosexual development as obscure and complicated; this idealogised the feminine in psychoanalysis.

In civilization a certain repression has taken place of the transmission of feminine enjoyment, the repression of those meeting-points between women that add up to erogeneity.

From this point of view the displacement of the erogenous zone (from the clitoris to the vagina) loses consistency and appears as a new artificial sacrifice that could be asked of the woman with a view to channelling the supposed normal path of her sensuality. As I understand it, this theorization of clitoral anaesthesia versus vaginal orgasm over-homologates feminine eroticism to masculine. It impoverishes the understanding of feminine sexuality and under the guise of explaining it, submerges it in that "dark continent" of which Freud speaks in *The Question of Lay Analysis* (1926e).

Marie Bonaparte (1949), a pioneer of psychoanalysis, is trenchant; this is what she says:

> The clitoris, woman's small phallus, must follow the lot of those temporary organs such as the thymus, which after having fulfilled this function for a transitory period, must succumb to involution.

Further on, she adds:

> Nevertheless, the most notable biological realisation of the feminine organism is precisely the power to direct the clitoral libido, which is a masculine force, and its maximum expression, orgasm, to the cloacal vagina, and this transference is sometimes so complete that the clitoris remains insensible. Then the woman with orgastic vaginal possibilities often overcomes the man, since it would appear that ultravaginal

women are precisely those in whom orgasm is produced with the greatest ease and intensity.

As one of her own symptoms, Flem (1986) relates that one of her reasons for consulting Freud in 1925 was to achieve normality in orgasm. In the quotation from Marie Bonaparte, "overcoming the man" and "ultravaginal" are expressions that resound with competitive connotations in the sphere of a phallic stage maintained at any cost, in which the collapse of the narcissistic shields attributed to the penis–phallus has not taken place.

Without abandoning the initial technical positions, later works of Marie Bonaparte take a different turn. She allocates a more relevant place to the "diffuse caresses" in the expansion of femininity.

Françoise Dolto (1982), referring to orgasm in women, distinguishes, following precise neuro-physiological paths, four distinct orgasms: clitoral, clitoro–vulvar, vulvo–vaginal, and utero–anexial. She attributes precise dynamics to each, declaring that the last (utero–anexial orgasm) is the best, or the most satisfying. Utero–anexial orgasm ". . . is mistakenly confused with the preceding orgasms, especially with vulvo–vaginal orgasm, because it is not consciously experienced by the woman, and therefore she never mentions it".

With so much labelling of the stages of sexuality and distinguishing between erogenous phenomena, we lose the dimension of instinctual richness, the interweaving of the erogenous zones, that characterizes the feminine way of achieving pleasure. Schemas attempt to circumscribe a sensitive–erogenous–emotional experience that cannot be described by schemes which demand an exact and unique formalization.

Transference: a sort of regression and repression

It is interesting to consider the three psycho-corporeal methods described by Freud (1905d) to account for the arrival at feminine sexuality that begins with the metamorphoses of puberty: a "sort of regression", repression, and transference. The woman's erogenous body must modify its function-dynamics, must abandon some ways of obtaining pleasure in order to stumble upon others and discover the vagina. Even if it does not explain what type of regression is referred to, it is possible to apply it to the idea of a regression to the primal erogenous matrix described earlier, and to evoke the thalassic regression studied so elegantly by Ferenczi (1924) in his investigation of the intensity of devolution in an act of love. Freud (1905d) seems to attribute this regression specifically to the woman. He writes: "Since the new sexual aim assigns very different functions to the two sexes, their sexual development now diverges greatly. That of males is the more straightforward and more understandable, while that of females actually enters upon a kind of involution" (p. 207).

Another mechanism that affects the body is the repression of the excitation of the clitoris. This point is fairly debatable. Although Freud was limited in his statement, its redeeming feature is, as I understand it, the implicit idea of a radical change in the perception of the erogenous sensations. Concentration on a single organ (clitoris) is abandoned to make possible the diffusion of eroticism. The clitoris becomes one more source of voluptuousness, not the main or only one. This polemic aspect of feminine sexuality is the fruit of a biased theory that proclaims that the woman must forget the excitability of the clitoris, that part or "piece of masculine sexuality" (Freud, 1905d, p. 221). As I understand it, there would be no repression of masculine sexuality in the woman, as Freud maintains, but silence on all things masculine (based on the resolution of phallic competence), which disappears as a useless remnant on the arrival at feminine eroticism. The clitoris, which is also feminine, transfers its erogeneity to other zones, which are ready to play their part freely and activate the experience of giving oneself a body. As far as transference is concerned, it is a very important erogenous movement. To transfer means to displace. The vagina "learns to feel" in various ways. From the theory of the cloaca it is not difficult to venture that everything "between the legs" of a woman is the source of many pleasures. It is a bodily area rich in erogenous zones and secretions: fluid, blood, faeces, urine. . . . There is transference from different zones, both from the clitoris and from other previously eroticized zones such as the anus and the breasts. Freud uses a fine image to refer to this transmission: ". . . just as . . . pine shavings can be kindled in order to set a log of harder wood on fire" (1905d, p. 221).

Luquet-Parat (1973) writes: "From the point of view of erogeneity, the anal phase is rich and complex and its resonance is great on future feminine sexuality. Passive cloacal erogeneity duplicates, from a certain moment, oral erogeneity before succeeding it" (p. 115).

Note also the important contribution of Lou Andreas-Salomé (1916) about the so-called "letting" of the anus to the vagina. All these contributions emphasize the multiplicity of ways that combine to awaken the excitability of the vagina.

To these so to say "classical" transferences, mouth–penis–clitoris–vagina (Jones, Klein, Freud) and anus–vagina (Lou Andreas-Salome), many variations can be added, to the extent that the whole body participates in its orificial and epidermic aspects, in its folds and windings and the combination of its sensorial aspects. The desiring flesh is now limited, now exceeded. Possibly a certain increase of sexual repression—a so-called "organic repression" (Freud, 1930a)—takes place, especially, as Freud pointed out, the intensity of the sexual barriers (modesty, repugnance, etc.) in little girls and their greater tendency to sexual repression (1905d).

In the changing times of puberty, the libido receives a new boost, and we become more and more aware of the vagina. With menstruation it receives the stimuli of the passing of the menstrual fluid. Not only does the vagina receive "transferences". New zones become erogenous, the skin becomes more receptive to caresses, the activation of phantasies weaves a representational and affective fabric over the activated erogenous matrix. All these are "shavings" that light the fire of the next sensual journey, until one reaches, in the state of enjoyment, the greatest indiscrimination and the highest point of representational annihilation. Transference will have been converted into a massive and total diffusion.

A field of desires, phantasies, promises, and illusions is taking shape. The body experiences voluptuousness itself, through the effects of conscious and unconscious ideas and the evocation of emotions. A memory, a furtive meeting with someone with a suggestive name, a feature that appeals by association with the primal object, following the trail of the forbidden and longed-for incest, are all sparks that stoke the fire of sensuality and transfer instinctual energy according to the heterogeneous complexity of every woman individually.

Even though the awakening of the senses encourages instinctual licence, it is known that what produces pleasure can be considered forbidden, and then mechanisms arise that seek to put a brake on this budding exuberance by generating various inhibitions or by erecting a barrier of disaffection (McDougall, 1989, chs. 6 and 7) in defence of the sleeping body.

Ferenczi (1924), in his original book *Thalassa*, makes important contributions. He postulates the fusion of eroticism into a superior unity—a process that he calls amphimixis. One eroticism lends its energy to another (the bladder to the anus, etc.), combining in search of discharge. He describes simultaneous eroticisms and various displacements like the interweaving of the senses (coloured hearing, acoustic vision, hearing by smell, etc.). The various transferences and summaries of eroticisms do not respond to any known physiological substrate. He even postulates the possibility of a multiplicity of forms of energy and mechanisms to account for the vicissitudes of erotic life because their ways of appearing are multifaceted and puzzling. A proof of this is the coenaestheses and processes in which the excitation of one receptor organ provokes the hallucinatory excitation of another. The investigations of Daniel Stern (1985) follow this line. He has studied the perceptive vicissitudes in the suckling's life, recognizing correspondences between different senses (e.g. touch and sight, p. 71.) He considers these transmodal equivalences to constitute the innate basis of the perceptive system in which transferences of information take place which alternately fuse and discriminate perceptions of different orders arising from various sources. Starting from these discoveries, the study of sensuality can be enriched, taking into consideration the effects produced by the alternation of various sensorial and emotional perceptions on the flow of the senses, causing now juxtapositions, now indiscriminations. In this way, perhaps, it is easier to understand that certain fusions of eroticisms impede the exact localization of the erogenous source, or that they multiply to fuse together in a higher unity, producing unexpected diffuse voluptuous effects or migratory localizations.

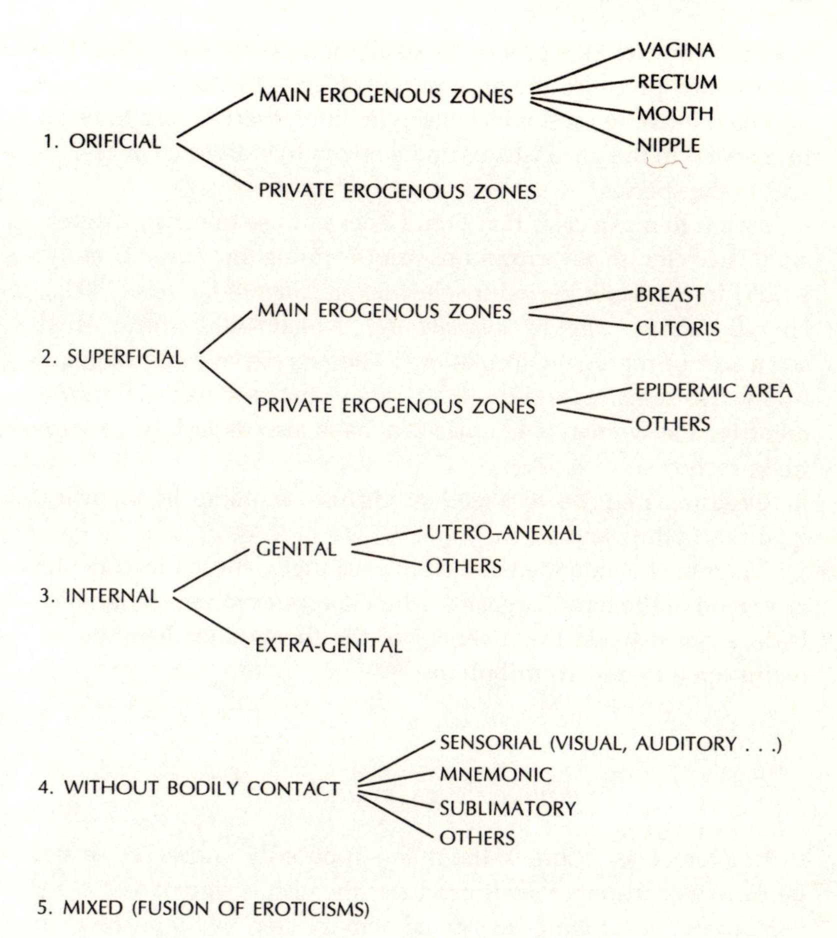

DIAGRAM 1. *Feminine orgasms*

The world of the senses does not follow a simple line. In erotic experiences that touch upon feelings of enjoyment in which impossible reality appears, precise categorizations, sexological exactness, and measurability are abandoned (see Diagram 1).

We are in the area of regression, that "species of regression" which Freud attributed specifically to women in 1905. More recently Ferenczi has something to add, referring to the thalassic regression (*Thalassa,* in Greek, means sea). This regression indicates a return to the ontogenetic and phylogenetic origins. The sea is a metaphor for "the past ocean of all mothers" in which lies "the calm which precedes the appearance of life". In this journey undertaken in coitus, and which sleep imitates, there is said to be an immersion in the unconscious and a return to individual ancestors and to the species.

I want to make clear that Freud does not use the term "regression" to refer to an erogenous transforming movement, as he would in the same period in *The Interpretation of Dreams* (1900a). He talks about *"eine Art Rückbildung"*, which could be translated as "a sort of regressive formation". The regressive sense of going backwards remains, and the specificity of the psychosexual movement for the woman is emphasized, as is also its lack of conceptual precision.

Orgasms may be localized or diffuse, variable in intensity, quality, rhythm, and so on.

Diagram 1 is intended as a simple arrangement to illustrate the extension of the term "orgasm" when it applies to the "feminine". It does not exhaust the diversity of the theme and therefore remains open to new contributions.

Feminine orgasm and men

If the woman is ignorant, the man supposedly knows. In sexual performance the erect penis produces the visible sign of eroticism. Sometimes, controlling his sexual activity step by step, the man carries out his directing role impeccably: erection, stimulation of the woman in order that she may obtain her orgasm, ejaculation.

It is a happy equation when the sexual companion combines elements of penetrating erotic vigour with a great display of tenderness. This allows the woman to find in him resonances of the primal mother-object or echoes of the "preferred form" (a smooth and powerful maternal perfection). Bisexuality can thus be most easily expanded. However, for the man to be tender may be considered to be the expression of a feminine trait. To this fear of becoming feminine is added another: that of taking part in a woman's erogenous overflow. Because of this, defensively, he may perhaps carry to extremes the control of his companion's sexuality or affect a certain violence through which his masculinity remains assured. (Maria tells us during a session how her flamboyant husband suddenly turned her away with a slap when she was about to have her first orgasm, thus causing her to become frigid from that moment on.) The frigid woman thus calms the man's fear of castration, confirming the difference of the sexes and guaranteeing his narcissistic integrity.

On the other hand, "the little girl appears to have more need of tenderness" (Freud, 1905d). This leads to what de Vilaine-Montefiore (n.d.) proposes: "And if men made love as we give the breast, feeding us with the liquid of life, penetrating us tenderly, maternally, profoundly. . . . His desire, his erection, not like a violation, a violence done to nature, to life, to an offering, but like a betrothal. . . ."

This exercise of tenderness is unconsciously opposed by many men in whom femininity engenders fear. Horror of genitals without a penis, that wound open to castration, meant that "the Devil took to flight when the woman showed him her vulva" (Freud, 1940c [1922], p. 274). Because in her enjoyment she speaks to the man of his death—an intolerable evocation. What makes her enjoy so excessively? What hidden secret? Will she die, will she go mad? She will be branded with nymphomania, she will have uterine fever, *vade retro*. . . . Once again the sinister, the demonic, the unnamed make their appearance.

The man will not be spared imagining himself as castrated nor risking the phantasms of bisexuality if he is to accompany a woman on her sensual journey.

Tenderness, "bisexual" preliminary pleasure, with both force and sweetness, masculine and feminine, is an antechamber to deep pleasures and access to enjoyment. To avoid these exciting experiences, there is often recourse to a sexual mechanism in which the first thing is for the woman to have an orgasm and the man to ejaculate. The woman, also afraid, lends herself to this scheme and offers her genitals so that the sexual discharge and the necessary interchange of secretions as one more physiological activity may take place as briefly as possible. The popular expression with which various women whom I have seen in a hospital service refer to their sexual life: "My husband *uses* . . . *so* many times a week"—clearly expresses their passive position and how they have detached themselves from their erogenous body, which they look on as an appendage, to be switched on while—as in a case that I remember vividly—the woman, during coitus, thought about the food she had to buy the next morning.

Here there is no journey to the dark continent, nor thalassic regression, nor experience of the uncanny. There is pleasure and a peaceful fulfilment of sexual obligations.

The other variant is the phantasm of the woman's "infinite orgasm" (Cournut, 1977) and the fears that it generates in the man. It gives the woman the status of demon and witch, as numerous references in literature and folklore attest. The man observes with terror the passage of enjoyment over a woman's body. "Tell me what it was like where you were, from where I thought you would never come back" is a possible enquiry ventured by a man who has questioned his own femininity.

Phantasies of erogenous overflow, fear of the uninhibited freedom of the senses, will cause much frigidity and problems with ejaculation or impotence, and "... it is thus that for tranquillity a large number of women enjoy like men, in little strokes or great gusts, in proportion to the masculine orgasm" (Cournut, 1977).

I want to take up one point again: femininity is not only a matter for women. And a man, incited by the erogenous richness of the woman, will have to accompany her on her regressive road, identifying himself with her in her orgasmic capacity and appealing to his own bisexuality. Thus to his phallic enjoyment he will add a supplement of sensual delights ... and what is more, transformed into Tiresias for an instant, he will be able to glimpse the magic emotional erogenous universe that is the feminine world.

Thus Rodrigué (1987) in a short story describes an erotic experience in which "the moment of orgasm having arrived, a diffuse enjoyment took its place". He calls this "different orgasm" in the man "woman's orgasm", accounting for the perception of sensualities of a different order.

Transgression (Bataille)

The concept of "transgression" occupies a privileged place in the theoretical part of the work of Bataille (1957). Subsequent contributions by Foucault (1963) enriched it, and later psychoanalysts

(Dorey, 1983, and Pérard, 1983, among others) began to take it up, seeking links between its original philosophical roots and its possible equivalents in psychoanalytic science.

Transgression is a happening that is *neither positive nor negative;* it is simply a phenomenon that is present in the order of experience. It has nothing to do with anything scandalous or subversive, and that means that it "is not animated by the potency of the negative" (Foucault, 1963). Further on he adds: "Nothing is negative in transgression. It affirms the limited being and the unlimited, into which it breaks, opening it for the first time to existence."

Transgression is defined as an interior movement based on pure experience, by means of which it is possible to look at the real, the impossible, the overflowing, the limitless. The greatest experiences in which it takes part are erotic experience, mystical experience, and artistic (creative) experience. It also appears in masochistic experience and in extreme experiences: emptiness, death, laughter, losses—experiences of catastrophe. It is an inner experience that reveals the possible relationship between finiteness and being.

Transgression occurs in much inner movement, only to disappear the next instant. The relationship between prohibition and transgression may be imagined as a framework in which the possibility of making any cuts does not exist. In their intimate intricacy, the prohibited and the transgressive (Foucault would say "limit" instead of prohibition) avoid all oppositional structures (yes and no, white and black, etc.). One is a condition of the other. Therefore "the relationship which transgression maintains with the prohibited, or, better still, with the limit, must be understood as the irreducible co-existence of opposed elements without any possibility of either transcending or synthesis" (Dorey, 1983).

The movement of transgression that gives entry to the transgressive experience is a copy of what happens with jokes (Freud 1905c); repression is abruptly lifted, only to be immediately reinstalled. It is not known exactly what one is laughing at, but in this laughter an effect materializes resulting from the meshing of a psychic movement composed of successive dynamics. In transgression, Bataille tells us, prohibition is lifted without being suppressed. As Dorey (1983) points out, this mechanism, to which the

German term *aufheben* applies perfectly, is difficult to translate in its verbal acceptance of "to lift while maintaining". In the interplay of transgression and limit, the limit transgressed keeps in potency the return to the first state as though it were a disorder in which two forces co-exist and which simply carry out an operation that splits the meshing into its two participating elements.

In creative experience, transgression shows its proximity to sublimation—the death of paternal authority, the impulse towards the maternal (Mother-Nature, said Freud in his *Leonardo*), looking for secrets to be unlocked. In the force that grasps the limit we can glimpse the origin of the creative act. There are resonances of sensuality in what I have just described, since all unleashing of the senses in the context of an erotic experience brings to the fore creativity in the discovery in one's own body of newness in the loved one, like an echo. Eroticism has a sublime aspect on the one hand, and on the other the potentiality to become infinite, inexhaustible.

Feminine sensuality, unfolding its erotic abundance, works in transgression, opening to the disturbed flesh in its excessive overflow, bringing the experience of ecstasy, which links the erotic with mysticism.

It is in this sensuality that the limit can move further and further away, where transgression can go to places that are more and more distant from what is known and nearer to the knot of the existentialist problem of the human being: to be or not to be, to live–to die. Death itself, in its concrete aspect, is not what is in play, but the experience of annihilation carried into the open spaces by the experience of depersonalization, of surrender, of representational–affective overflow, of flooding by excess. The feminine in excess, overflowing, is watered down in not-being.

At the maximum of surrender, in the depths of ecstasy, there is here the overcoming of horror, and access, from sensual exuberance and multiple enjoyment, to the borders of reality. Amid the rough paths trodden by the feeling of nothingness, ecstasy based on the dangerous act of transgressing speaks of the defiant boldness of a subject in a state of desire. Freudian desire (Dorey, 1983) shows its transgressive character. The desire of the Other sets limits, which the subject, with her transgression, displaces to give birth to thought and language.

In erotic transgressive experience, eroticism touches on mysticism when the overflow of enjoyment gives the subject access to the inner experience of oceanic fusion, of return to the origins, of dissolution of consciousness. In the shattering and transitory capture of the impossible, in the cessation of the One which happens in the crossing to the nameless and the indiscriminate, are the propitious elements for the advent of the sacred sentiment. The sacred element shines immersed in impropriety, in the vastness of an unlimited experience, the fruit of the transgressive path to the unknown beyond the senses, when in its joyful flowering the force of desire overwhelms all that is known, simply leaving naked a disturbed flesh that knows nothing, that is nothing. Then the serious element takes shape, in that close contact with mystery, in the intervention of the universe of enigmas. The body emerges entire. Transgression has imprinted on its flesh the experience of the intimate fusion between life and death.

Some popular expressions relating to erotic life betray the links between the erotic and religious experience: "I saw God", "I rose to Heaven", or, in French, *"Tu me mets aux anges"* [You put me among the angels].

The experience itself, bordering on the ineffable and the incomprehensible, makes it difficult to define transgression. This leads Dorey (1983) to say that the psychoanalytic conception of the term has not been completed, since transgression "speaks from another place and in a different way: I would even say that it sets us in motion rather than speaking to us, that we live it rather than understand it. It is perhaps the reason why its true being appears to escape from all conceptual appreciation."

The transgression-limit movement is an experience in which risk and challenge play a part, or the boldness of penetrating the territory of the known in order to free it and give place to the unexpected. In the violence that is inherent in it, tumult manifests itself and challenge insinuates itself into anxiety. The being presents itself in its sudden and evanescent character in those single possible acts of exploration of life and exploration of death. The abolition of the subject forms part of the working of transgression. In the multiplicity of transgressive experiences, the outstanding one is "being without truce"—a poetic, glowing phrase of Bataille's that lets us glimpse the edifying value of this movement in its disalienating state and in the space of truth that it establishes.

As Foucault writes (1963):

> Nothing is more alien to her than the figure of the demonic which "denies everything". Transgression opens on to a sparkling world, and always in affirmation, a world without shade, without twilight, without that sliding denial that damages fruits and injects into their hearts its own contradiction. It is the solar reverse of Satanic negation, it forms part of the divine, or rather opens, from that limit which indicates the sacred, the space in which the divine unfolds.

I thought it relevant to introduce this notion of transgression before referring in detail to the complexity of feminine orgasms and the obstacles that the feminine erogenous flesh evades and leaps over in reaching the paroxysm of the senses and its final dumbness or destruction. The experiences of the body instigate and encapsulate the adventure of life and death that is involved in every truly erotic experience.

The term "transgression" has acquired specificity ever since Bataille's developments appeared, and to make its true importance clear it is important to remember them.

Feminine orgasms

I want to bring out the different lines along which this theme can be expanded. I begin by leaving the floor to a young analysand whose expressions take us into the very heart of the problem.

She says:

> "A man passes and I look at him. A woman passes and I look at her. . . . I see a naked woman, and I can become excited and it makes me doubt my femininity. . . . Sometimes it seemed to me that I had a penis; at secondary school I put on baggy trousers and the pelvic bone was very prominent. . . . I remember that it was as though I had a penis. . ."

> "Mama said that I had a tail in front and a tail behind. I knew nothing about the vagina. . . . The first time I put in a tampon, I

> did not really know where I had to put it or how—it made me hot and anxious. I was ashamed that I did not know where the vagina was. . . . And the fear when my breasts began to grow, one before the other, and I had just one breast, I nearly died—it was as though I were deformed."

Further on:

> "The very intense feeling all over my body, as though there were other orgasms, but it was important to get to the big one, the others were sort of half worn away, one loses force, I always devalued the less intense orgasms, as though instead of the great orgasm the small one is poorer. . . . The thing saddens me. Besides, for me . . . I analysed an idea and came to the conclusion that the penis is the greatest thing in the world, and magical, as if I felt that in some way that was never going to change, because I am still convinced that men are superior."

Penis-envy, the ignorance of the vagina, the female bodily scheme, and the displacement of the penis to the orgasm are emphasized. It can be observed how the masculine way of reaching orgasm (huge, very male) impregnates a woman's phantasies. They are orgasms preceded by important previous steps: erection, spasmodic movements, ejaculatory explosion, refractory period following the detumescence of the penis, emission of semen. There is then talk of women who during orgasm secrete a great quantity of fluid—"almost like an ejaculation"—or who when they reach the orgasm remain exhausted and totally insensible, as though they had been affected by the detumescence of the penis. Even the cry of the woman in orgasm is said to be the support or guarantee that "that" has happened. The feminine orgasm is thus mirrored in the myth of the sexual functioning of the male. And one woman will want to have an orgasm as another has dreamed of having a penis. She seeks that which is tangible, important, localizable, repressing her erotic perceptions and the self-delighting part of her eroticism.

In what is heard in analysis (as shown by the vignette above) there appears as it were a complaint of an absence, a lament about something missing in the act of love, or something obtained after difficult "sexual work". There is a clear phantasy of a lack, in opposition to women who would have it according to an orgasm–phallus equation.

On other occasions, in symptomatic silence, the woman keeps back all association related to the changes in her desiring body. On the one hand it is a pure narcissistic mirage, although on the other, in complaints or questions about orgasm, the woman is also questioning herself about her femininity, which may lead to "pretending" orgasm or believing that what happens is it. Her pretence betrays the complexity of the search for her erogenous path.

The fact that penis-envy comes into play is expressed in different ways in a woman's erotic intimacy. In the case of the frigid woman, it may be that she is claiming her phallic triumph in the face of a partner who is unable to fulfil her with enjoyment. Much has been written about the body as a phallus, the bodily stiffness with which a frigid woman "tolerates" lovemaking, symbolizing the erect penis. In other cases, she maintains in an unalterable virginity her phantasized victory over castration. It also happens that the orgasm comes only at the precise instant at which the man ejaculates, exactly on the detumescence of the penis. Orgasm for orgasm, it is a condition of pleasure that the penis should become flaccid.

We often see women "despairing" at their lack of pleasure, going from one sexual object to another, with the illusion that they will meet the man who will teach them about themselves, who will introduce them to their feminine condition, who will try to divest them of the unconscious rivalry, which is like armour-plating in their approach to femininity.

In the case of my patient, it can be seen how—beyond the great orgasm—there opens a space that is defensively devalued. In the supposed and disappointing "small orgasm" there lies the possibility of abandoning oneself to a different libidinal movement.

Putting aside the phallus as enchantment, what remains to the feminine being? A new field, through which emptiness insinuates itself, a space to be crossed by a necessary leap so that one can show oneself, dodge the precipice of castration, and fling one's body into a nameless adventure, in a sort of regression, a depersonalizing experience in which random and contingent elements play a part. It is where one can approach a different capacity for enjoying the body.

* * *

I believe that it is a good idea to introduce here the distinction between pleasure and enjoyment, and their link with the various orders of instincts. Freud said that the psychic apparatus was a "tireless seeker after pleasure", like a magnet, so to speak, attracting the possible objects of satisfaction. To distinguish between pleasure and enjoyment, we have to consider that pleasure is always an effect of partial instinct (Sciarreta, 1986) even when its source is the genital organ whose primacy is the sexual function.

Enjoyment, on the other hand, is put into action by the death instinct and implies an instinct that involves the whole body, "and which has a negative character which implies finiteness and limitation with which there may be something like anticipation of death" (Sciarreta, 1986). Enjoyment goes in search of a plenitude that on an imaginary plane tends to be absolute.

The instincts, riding on the senses, aspire to gratification. The interlacing of the instincts decides the destiny of the discharge and its quality, and the various combinations show the predominance or the relative lack of an instinct.

In human erotic life, enjoyment emerges closely linked to a sort of experience of natural death—a little death or fine death—in the immersion in voluptuous waves in which the identity is lost for a more or less brief instant, but from which it revives jubilantly. Representations are effaced, and language acquires a primal character.

Preliminary pleasure constitutes at one and the same time the source of discharge of partial instincts and the antechamber to enjoyment, in that it is the entrance to the harmony of the senses, which, combined with the instincts (of life, of death), moves in accordance with the erogenous rhythm of every subject and the special circumstances of every situation towards the regions of a greater pleasure.

The human subject fears the unfolding of enjoyment, since it involves experiences of depersonalization. For that reason one often finds an absence of enjoyment in both men and women; they show a clear preference for the experiences of a simple, controlled pleasure, which is also, on the other hand, extremely gratifying.

But power over control is a pure Utopia. Passion may surprise and transport to a greater or lesser extent. And besides, the call of desire confronts the subject with that impossible *objet à* about which Lacan has so much to say.

Taking up again the woman's changes of experience as regards her erogeneity, I wish to repeat (the woman's bisexuality was strongly brought out by Freud) that the woman enjoys in two ways. On the one hand, she takes part in the virile way of enjoying, with her clitoris, her vagina, her erotic concentration on the cathexis of a single organ, her phallic illusion, even in identification with the man. On the other hand, she enjoys in the feminine way, with the hidden, the indefinable, the phantasy of origins, thalassic regression, the diffusion of eroticism, bodily illegality. Melanie Klein (1975, p. 205) has emphasized that the woman tends to attach her narcissism to her body as a whole, "distributing it to a greater extent over the whole of her body" due to her various bodily functions and excretory processes, whereas the man focuses his narcissism on his genitals.

Enjoyment strictly speaking is not forbidden to the woman. She can have a well-localized, sexologically measurable orgasm, with an abundant secretion that imitates semen. Now to limit feminine pleasure to that form implies leaving aside a very great range of crucial erogenous and affective phenomena in the unfolding of the wealth of her erotic potential.

The woman may know erogenous delights independent of topological discrimination. The erogenous zones are displaced and turn their erogeneity over to each other, thus forming a sort of total "bath of erogeneity". In addition, stories, legends, memories, affective experiences, intermediary mnemonic tracks (at the level of representation and at the level of affect) all generate libidinization or unique and particular *private erogenous zones* for a certain subject at a given period of life.

Annie Anzieu (1987, p. 141) has stressed the confusion of zones as characteristic of hysteria, in which oral excitation is displaced to other zones of the body, such as the skin or the sensorial orifices; she maintains that the confusion between mouth and sex determines feminine sexual perversions and incapacities. I include this contribution to make clear that that which in hysteria shows a specific zonal displacement in the service of erotic anaesthesia, surprises in the non-hysterical woman by its plasticity and mobility and the creation of particular new erogenous zones. A double configuration takes shape regarding feminine sensuality: in the first, precise recognition appears of both the main and the minor erogenous zones (Freud, 1905d). Here we are approaching the territory of the particular sensibilities of each woman, her preferred caresses, movements, and environmental contexts favourable to the stimulation of her eroticism. The second configuration is to be found on the opposite path: precisions are blurred, and eroticisms blend and intermingle. In that harmony of pleasures, enjoyment finds a place to extend. Precise pleasures co-exist with movements of regression and depersonalization in which exactitude and exact localization disappear. As the woman lacks a penis in terms of possessing a directing organ that must fulfil precise physiological demands in the sexual act, and as the phantasm of tangible impotence does not appear in her (she knows that she can hide frigidity), this makes the man so vulnerable in his narcissism when it is a question of love-prowess that the woman can show this form of imprecise enjoyment which results from a sum of perceptive and sensitive eroticism. Ferenczi's concept of the amphimixis of eroticisms (mentioned above)—which designates the fusion of two or more eroticisms in a superior unity—may be applied here, with the reservation that all the eroticisms would not flow only into the genital organ (the vagina in this case) but would discharge one with the other in multiple combinations.

The woman will have to extricate herself from the demands of the superego and the oedipal rivalries to let her desiring flesh unfold the sensitive–affective–erogenous variables that are proper to her. As she loses all ordering models of what she must come to feel, there remains uncovered a lack of knowledge, and the door opens to a dimension of unknown sensualities that disturb because they are unforeseeable and because they do not conform to traditional canons, nor to what might be expected of her sensuality, if it is to be in accordance with cultural guidelines.

When the woman's body relaxes and enters into a state of enjoyment, her general appearance becomes frightening—her overflow draws infinity on her flesh. She is like a witch at an orgy, at a witches' Sabbath of the senses, with its instinctual disorder and ecstasy. Orgasms cannot be measured nor counted, the number is not important, the measurement laughs at the exactitude of all measuring, the flesh is confused, disordered, submerged in its bath of unconsciousness and dreams. The immeasurable wildness recreates a mythical state of "before birth" beyond the universe of language. Sensibility may reach a point at which it turns to the dissolution of sensibility, a fall from the body, detachment from oneself. Perceptive faith (Merleau-Ponty, 1945) is lost, the senses deceive, but none of it matters. It is the hour of ecstasy and of self-dispossession.

Lacan (1972–1973) conceptualizes feminine enjoyment, which he calls "enjoyment in excess" or "extra enjoyment", enjoyment "beyond the phallus". It is an enjoyment that does not derive from the phallus. I want to transcribe a paragraph from his seminar. He says: "There is an enjoyment from her to herself which does not exist and which means nothing. There is an enjoyment in her of which perhaps she knows nothing either, but which she experiences—that she knows—she knows it, of course, when that happens to her. That does not happen to all women."

Lacan stresses the ineffability of feminine enjoyment, which belongs to a realm in which it co-exists with the secret, the untransferable, and the unsayable. He also shows that this enjoyment goes beyond its pertinence to the species of woman, since its advent depends on fortuitous circumstances. Women can be divided artificially into those who have access to excessive enjoyment and those to whom it is denied. The first category—"woman–women", as it is usually said in order to emphasize the femininity of a woman—are those who touch on witchcraft and mysticism, those who deal with God and the devil, those who fly from their bodies to unknown regions, those who incarnate the real. It is not too bold to consider that when it is a question of enjoyment—that is, experiences that transcend the level of words through which affective and phantasmatic archaisms are glimpsed—the logic of knowledge is suspended, and all *a posteriori* construction of the experience will always be insufficient to express the richness and profusion of sensitive and erogenous nuances that have taken place. Like a dream, the essential, the famous nucleus is beyond the precision of words. This happens with all enjoyment, not only with feminine enjoyment, given that the participation of the death instinct decathectizes, disobjectivizes (Green, 1986), pushes towards the return to the inorganic, and so removes what was personally experienced thanks to her, the higher functions of conscience and memory.

In regressive experience of enjoyment things are revived that happened in the early days—the space of the primal orgasm is recreated. The surrender, introducing the dimension of the principle of Nirvana, brings into play a total pleasure that takes in the whole body.

Expressions of fear of lack of control or madness may appear. M says: "If it lasts a long time, I believe one could go mad." Another patient says: "I trembled all over, right to the skin" when describing an outpouring of love. It is useless to try to specify one part of the body. The whole body had trembled on the desirous contact with the body of a man.

For the woman it is possible for the whole body to become an erogenous zone in which senso-perceptive waves and diffuse billows of voluptuousness develop like multiple epicentres. To the mythical uproarious orgasm in the masculine way (which on the other hand also happens to a woman's body) is added the joyful surface of an erogenous affective body, which is permanently rediscovering itself—the source of small, medium, or great orgasms. There is no law to stipulate how we achieve access to pleasure and enjoyment. And besides, there is a point in the orgasm that it is impossible to map. Every woman goes as far as she can with her body.

If the dimension of enjoyment is deeper and more regressive than that of pleasure, it is also certain that it is nearer to suffering. I want to recall thus the simple dominance of pleasure, the satisfactory revitalizing relief, the pleasant experience that removes actual neurosis.

Orgasm may be oral, anal, visual, tactile, auditory, clitoral, vulvar, vaginal. As they flow, orgasms expand capriciously through the body, sketching an arbitrary map of changing and unexpected erogenous zones.[3]

Orificial orgasms (unleashed by the main internal sensitive zones such as the vagina, the rectum, and the mouth) can be distinguished from surface orgasms (external, sensitive) in which the combination of sensorial stimuli and, above all, skin contacts play a fundamental role.

From the feminine sexual expansion every erogenous zone is liable to be converted into a discharge area and provoke that "sort of orgasm" (Freud, 1905d) followed by voluptuousness, deep satisfaction, and a growing disposability to pleasure.

The woman who has surrendered does not know herself or ask herself. Spaces have opened to her, and she penetrates them in her turn (feminine penetration) without demands or expectations, without needing to pinpoint precisely the places where she obtains pleasure or enjoyment, without measure, without verifiable sexual product, without a single mechanism of discharge. This "without" is essentially feminine. It is a "without" that refers to a completeness of a different order from narcissistic phallic completeness, a "without" that transcends narcissism and realizes the overcoming of castration.

While the man plays, with desire, on a woman's body, the feminine woman passively lets herself be penetrated, and in her turn penetrates with active passivity into an ever-changing space that leads her to a suspension of representations.

Feminine narcissism, penis-envy, the conflicts that usually disturb the feminine soul are temporarily suspended in that immersion in the unconscious, in that dream-voyage. That which under the rule of penis-envy would have been expressed as anaesthesia or an obstacle now receives the favours of a body submerged in the plenitude of want in a kind of journey to the unconscious, like an experience of disappearance and resurrection.

Erogenous masochism is part of the movement of dispossession, an imaginary acceptance of being dominated, invaded. Waves of erogenous masochism make the libido docile and introverted. It has its basis in the phantasm of the primal sado-anal scene, and identification with the mother is brought into the sexual act. At the same time, following Janine Chasseguet-Smirgel (1964), it appeases the sense of guilt in this delicious imaginary punishment for unconscious death-wishes. Nevertheless, the sadistic impulse and the exercise of dominance appear also in the capture of the penis in vaginal spasms.

Melanie Klein, in *The Psycho-Analysis of Children* (1975), stresses the gratification that ensues in the woman through the presence of the destructive components that surface during the sexual act.

It may be observed that the preliminary pleasure comes very near to the final pleasure as far as feminine orgasms are concerned. I would call "orgasms on a feminine body" the voluptuous discharges that take place in the play previous to penetration. These surface orgasms open the way to penetration orgasms. Thus we have different types of orgasmic expansion. It is possible that the word "orgasm" thus applied is confusing when we are automatically looking for the equivalent of the man's orgasm in the woman. Multiple erogenous discharges, waves of voluptuousness serve as synonyms for feminine orgasms.

Freud (1916–17) in his lecture on regression, observed that the instincts were "related to one another like a network of intercommunicating channels" in spite of their being subject to the primacy of the genitals; he added, "It is a state of affairs that is not at all easily combined in a single picture" (p. 345). With these words he demolished the rigid dividing line that he had established in *Three Essays* (1905d) between preliminary pleasure and final or genital pleasure.

Hasty labels of frigidity are due in many cases to ignorance of the multiplicity of feminine erogeneity. It is therefore reasonable to question certain investigations (Hite, 1987) that show statistically a very high percentage of frigidity in women. Do they not in fact mean that all these women are frigid with respect to a form of enjoyment that is expected of them, one of the male sort, and is it not true that labelling them in this way does not take into account that there exist forms of pleasure and enjoyment that do not conform to the masculine cliché, and which women themselves, when asked, disparage, considering that they do not deserve to be included in their erotic assets? Woman, trapped in the ideal valuation of a way of experiencing pleasure in the masculine style, discounts an essential part of her eroticism and inhibits her own libidinal movements.

In order to overcome the inevitable inhibitions and distances with which love-play begins, the important requirements in surrender may well be *a minimum of demand and a maximum of desire.* It is known besides that these journeys of pleasure and/or enjoyment may come to fruition gradually, by stages, in forms entirely idiosyncratic to each woman. The potentiality of the unforeseen will be present, bringing surprising new sensations. The condition of "letting go" presupposes this openness. The affective–erogenous body vibrates while the psychic apparatus retraces its mnemonic steps, suspends representations, to run into the sensorial perceptive pole, into the world of images, sounds, odours, rhythms, pressures, and so on, following the path of dreams Freud sketches in chapter VII of *The Interpretation of Dreams.*

Not only does the man fear the woman's excessive enjoyment—that enjoyment which triggers off the totalizing dimension of the death instinct in its depersonalizing role, as I have explained—but the woman also fears the unfolding of that desiring force which drags her out of herself and which unleashes a sort of regression whose outcome she cannot predict. Thus she will often try to control the role of erogenous zones by adopting neuroses, such as the masculinity complex, the rejection of all erotic life, seeking refuge in virginity or choosing a partner in tune with her defences.

The feminine erogenous transferential capacity inspires fear to the extent to which it implies biological disorder, instinctual anarchy, the passage from one place of excitation to another in a way that is often unforeseen, surprised by the effects when one zone of the body begins to give forth pleasure. Annie Anzieu (1987) presents an interesting vignette. She says:

> When Mrs G speaks of the pleasures of love, she evokes the fear which arouses in her the idea of possible orgasm and prevents her from consuming it. She refers to this as to a loss of herself, not a simple loss of consciousness; it is something which terrifies her like death. Reality does not exist for her except as a kind of dream, as Freud had already proved in other patients. The non-integration of the qualitative differences of the erogenous zones, of the mouth and the sex, in the ego, at the same time as the interior–surface, container–content indifferentiation, appear to be the sources of this confusion

> between dream and reality. The regression produced by the idea of penetration, always intrusive for Mrs. G, unleashed in her early paranoid fears of being destroyed from within. Pleasure is assimilated to death. [p. 135]

I must also point out that women themselves, arriving at the door of femininity, usually keep silent about their outrageous bodily adventures. Excess—this "too much" taking place momentarily in the flesh in a state of enjoyment—incarnates magical mysteries that make us think of legendary happenings, beyond the possible and the imaginable.

The well-known question "What does a woman want?" will remain unanswered. To ask a woman what she knows, what she can define, is to take her out of her feminine place. In any case, she will want to frighten away the paralysing oedipal phantasms in order to find the regressive path and give herself meekly into the arms of the man who would transport her into the hallucinated place of dispossession, an amorous ecstasy in which symbols fall away and there comes the submersion in a history for which only the unconscious can account. The narcissistic wound opened in the supposed humiliating castration of a body that is "deformed" or mutilated gives way to another meeting with the unconscious effects.

From Lacan's viewpoint, this can be thought of as the joining of the three registers, each offering distinct possibilities. With respect to the imaginary, the phastasms act like a dream, taking on images or sensitizing the body to receive unconscious emanations. Visual images, inarticulate voices, sounds referring to another unconscious "scene" will emerge. The symbolic level is expressed in the choice of a sexual object where there is a recognition of castration in that man, which is necessary for making love. The real shows in its turn the impossibility of going beyond the limits of the body; it defines the maximum enjoyment that can be reached through which the unsymbolized can be realized. It borders that which is behind the primal repression. This meeting with the real would explain the fear of madness or meeting a mangled part of the body. The capacity for orgasm is then abandoned with horror, in order to escape from an experience that is too sinister. On other occasions the body's pleasure may reach a certain point and then clash with the all-embracing narcissistic phantasm that resists incompleteness and prefers not to surrender, so as to seek enjoyment elsewhere, to the benefit of the phallic, complete man.

The richness of feminine orgasms embodies a problem of life and death that contradicts all narcissistic ideas about the immortality of the ego. The dissolution of the ego is facilitated by thalassic regression (Ferenczi, 1924), with the consequent experiences of annihilation and dispersion.

Bataille (1957) has written that "eroticism is the approval of life up to death", stressing the sense of elemental violence that resides in eroticism in preparing the fusion of lovers and its dissolution in a sort of abyss that "in one sense is death, and death is vertiginous, is fascinating" (p. 13). He distinguishes masculine from feminine, saying: "The passive part, feminine, is essentially that which dissolves in so far as it is constituted. But for a masculine participant the dissolution of the feminine part has only one sense: it prepares a fusion in which two beings are mingled who finally arrive together at the same point of dissolution." Here we see the adventure of sensuality that opens the door to the dream-voyage of eroticism. Inasmuch as we are isolated and discontinuous beings, each destined to die his own unique death, the experience of enjoyment with a fellow being is one of the ways that bring us back to continuity, which make it possible for us to plunge into the depths of the unconscious, relieve the anguish of solitude and return to the mythical paradise of the origins, to the womb, to a warm and secure psychic and physical space. Individuality is blurred, giving relief to that subject who manages to penetrate within the confines of his materiality. *The death instinct introduces one to Nirvana and is in the service of life.* On this point it separates decidedly from destruction; on the contrary, it facilitates regression to the state that is most similar to the inorganic one, when we cease to be one and become inseparable from the whole, supported by the image of the primal object. Thus the "little death" of orgasm is a good death, because (Chambon, 1977, p. 634) it refers to a death from which one is resuscitated—in other words, an antithesis of death. Nevertheless, if the orgasm is precise and limited, there will be a greater chance that the orgasm–death equation will not come about. There will be little enjoyment, and the bodies will not express their perishable nature. This also explains the preference for young bodies: the aesthetic element is combined with the phantasy of perpetual youth, which pushes away the representation of death.

The road that separates animals from man acquires the greatest importance. It is not a question of a primitive sexual interchange without language, without conflict, without barriers like modesty, disgust, and shame. Rather, it is a question of people with language who are capable of wonder about the sense of life rooted in a universe of ideals and values.

This led Bataille to distinguish in a masterly way between three types of eroticisms: that of bodies, that of hearts, and the sacred one. The eroticism of bodies was not the object of his greatest interest. He found in it something turgid and egotistical. The eroticism of hearts, on the other hand, "is freer" (p. 19). It includes the reciprocal emotion of lovers as a sacred eroticism that sees the sexual as symbolizing a higher union.

Obscenity intervenes in the service of the violence that is necessary in order to penetrate intensely into the other, in search of the flesh in its most repellent materiality (behind the naked body it shows the rotting corpse). It borders on a devastating reality, seeing death met again in the body. Continuity (fusion) is achieved through the crime of individuality.

In any case, there is a limit to what can be experienced. The lack, the shadow of the lost object and the spectre of death (Bérouti, 1977) are landmarks in sensual experience.

The nature—unsatisfactory in itself—of all experience of satisfaction was brought into relief in a note in Freud's "Findings, Ideas, Problems" (1941f [1938]), in which he refers to certain equivalents of orgasm such as crises of laughter or tears. He states there that there is always something missing for full discharge and satisfaction: *"en attendant toujours quelque chose qui ne venait point"* [always waiting for something that never comes].

Even in the fullest erogenous experience there is an element of incompleteness, and the subject is propelled by desire to set off again in search of the impossible, trying to find that interminable and inexhaustible "more still" which involves repetition and the unattainable longing for an indefinable archaic pleasure.

Orgasm does not make up for what is lacking. Desire is never extinguished. On the contrary, "the bringing into play of nostalgic aspiration in the process of orgasm maintains the possibility of returning to the lack. From this point of view, the death instinct, the accomplice of libido in the psychic process of orgasm, is the 'fundamental' guarantee against psychic death" (Bérouti, 1977).

There remains one mystery among many to be revealed: that of the famous "taming" of the instincts (Freud, 1937c), for the solution of which Freud appeals to witchcraft and even to a witch-metapsychology. The question that arises is how the most exquisite sensual intensities can be in the service of the most sublime aspects of a subject. The answer is not simple. It is not merely a matter of finding an object that is adequate to satisfy the demands of pleasure. The human link emerges in its dimension of altruism and respect. The law is made flesh. Sensuality penetrates into the higher values, and consideration for the other acquires relevance. To that other Freud gives the name of *Nebenmensch* in the *Project*, which literally means "human being at my side", my fellow being.

Notes

1. I am grateful to Dr. Juan Carlos Weissmann for confirming to me that the term "*Pollution*" in German is used strictly for masculine ejaculation. Similarly, he pointed out to me the wealth of nuances in the word *Liebeserguss* [overflow of love] used by Freud.

2. Klein (*The Psycho-Analysis of Children*, 1975) points out the psychic moment in which the prohibition of touching, displaced on to her internal genitals, falls on the little girl.

3. Not long after writing my works on the feminine orgasm (1988b and 1989), I discovered a 1952 work by Judd Marmor, which presents ideas similar to mine. I want to mention especially the section referring to extragenital orgasm in women, in which he quotes a study carried out by Dickinson and Beam on 1,000 marriages. From this study I quote the following: "Archives contain cases of orgasms achieved by sucking the nipples, by the fact of being side by side, by suckling the baby, by squeezing together (completely dressed), by having one's hair washed by a hairdresser, by a look, a kiss, touching the eye or the ear, a handshake, and by the fact of observing a picture or a flower which do not contain any figure or any similarity to any person or scene" (p. 253).

The notion of feminine orgasms is far from physiology; it borders on an almost spiritual erogeneity and shows a woman's capacity to relive the reflex act of orgasm in different equally pleasant situations, beyond all stimulation of the main erogenous zones. Reading "observing a picture or a flower", I think again of the "orgasms of the ego" described by Winnicott (1958) linked with sublimation and the capacity to be alone.

CHAPTER FOUR

Feminine virginities

> But is the unicorn a falsehood? It's the sweetest of animals and a noble symbol. It stands for Christ and for chastity; it can be captured only by setting a virgin in the forest, so that the animal, catching her most chaste odour, will go and lay its head in her lap, offering itself as prey to the hunters' snares.
>
> [Umberto Eco: *The Name of the Rose*, p. 315]

For what I have to say on feminine sensuality, "virgin" is written in the plural. The realm of the virgin is extensive; it includes the *state of virginity*, the realm of the closed and protected, *the movements of deflowering*, which in the form of disguises penetrate into the intimacy of the self, and the *process of reflowering*—amazing, complex, but no less certain.

The word "virgin" would seem to be the heritage of the woman. In classical Greek, the word *parthenos* is in the feminine gender and is used in the masculine only by analogy in the New Testament. Similarly, in Latin the word *virgo* is in the feminine gender. For the Church, virginity is deeply inscribed in the eternal nature of woman, a nature that is both biological and psychological at the same time. And the Gospel, which establishes Mary's virginity, does not allude once to the virginity of Joseph or Jesus (Hourcade, 1989).

According to psychoanalysis, the body and the psyche "speak" one upon the other. Their speech is sometimes distinct, sometimes superimposed one on the other. The virginity of the mind is mated with that of the body. A woman may have been deflowered and keep the status of virgin in the most deeply hidden part of her being, or, rather, using the term dear to Freud when referring to psychism, feel a virgin in the *soul* [*Seele*].

Eulogy of the virgin

The Larousse dictionary says about the word virgin: "person who has lived in perfect continence. The Virgin Mary. Fig.: something that is not smirched or mixed. Virgin forest: that which has never been exploited. Virgin land: that which has never been cultivated."

In the first place, she is the great generator. Here is the mother of gods, a restrained figure, mistress of herself, the flesh of an angel, the pure supporter of an ethical escutcheon, with her body deprived of an erogenous body, full of well-being, peace, and perfect balance. She is accompanied by the child born of a virgin, always a divine child, a saviour who emerges from a miraculous body, intermediary of the designs of a higher authority who regulates the order of the universe. All religions repeat this constant feature: the god is born of a virgin. "The myth of a god born of a virgin is found throughout the world, beginning with India, where Krishna was borne by a chaste virgin called Degald" (Monestier, 1963).

The inhabitants of ancient Mexico venerated a redeemer of the world called Quetzalcoatl, conceived by a virgin. The Chinese venerated Kwan–Yin; the Celts, the virgin who was to conceive; the Christians, Mary; the Hindus, Maha Shakti, "Divine Mother"; the gnostics, Sophia; the Jews, Miriam. Horus and Ra in Egypt also descended from a virgin. Zoroaster, in Persia (Lewis, quoted by Monestier, 1963), was the first redeemer of the world whose birth was recognized as originating in the immaculate conception of a virgin.

A high power uses a pure woman's body so that a God or a Son of God may come from her womb. The sensual interchange between the child and his virgin mother is immersed in the ambit of the immaculate, of the good. There is no dirt or blemish. The intimate mother–child fusion is an interchange in which all is permitted, a space of immense desirous interaction where body fluids do not stain and lochia, meconium, blood, urine, milk, faeces, saliva will sustain each other in the frame of a dignified bond. There has been no deflowering, there has been no injury, there is no trace of impurity in the copulation of bodies. The man has not touched her. There has been, on the other hand, an intervention from the sublime, the word of God, a great space for the unfolding of ideals, for a relieving order from a great authority. The gods, above humanity, maintain immortality, that which is for ever, the omniscience that calms the uncertain task of living. In the Virgin is order and obedience, annunciation and miracle. This idea of virginity that the religions present to us is poignant and ranges from ingenuousness to wisdom.

Virginity includes the concept of parthenogenesis. The son is a fruit of a sameness, a fruit of the intimate union of the subject with herself, of an intrapsychic eroticism, of a force of self.

The Virgin does not ask, receive, make, bear, and create a child, illuminated by narcissism on the altars of Eros. She is Woman with a capital W, valued to a high degree, her flesh protected from all humiliation.

She belongs to herself and is at the same time the instrument of a word that happily obeys. The ego-ideal and the ideal of the ego are fused, and "she" has access to a joy that transcends the sensuality of the flesh in the name of a joy of transcendence, of a divine order, to enjoy only her son and his acceptance.

I sketch a trophic concept of virginity which calls for a body–mind–soul that contains itself intact in its full potentiality. The hymen is "clasped", so to speak, to the subject and ensures his imaginary integrity.

The Virgin "is in herself". She does not depend on another mortal, nor does she scatter anxieties around the world. She delimits the space of inner integrity, the capacity to be fertile on her own, a tranquil creative potential, the blessed satisfaction of accepting a different order. There the symbolic ties itself in knots. The state of virginity at its symbolic level is closely related to the taming of the instincts and the mediation of desire.

Virginity structures the erogenous body. It is the law made flesh. Not all is valid in the interchanges of desire, and one can set a limit on the rules of the game of pleasure and love. This is the fierce aspect of virginity, which constitutes an imperative.

Virginity is all the more precious because it is in the realm of difficult achievements. One takes a psychic hymen for oneself, belongs to oneself, gives to oneself. The intersubjective becomes intrasubjective, and in virginity the psychic instances act synchronously.

The state of virginity implies a self-covering that has resulted from an almost surgical psychic act of severance from the common skin of the mother.

In eulogizing the virgin, from the point of view of psychoanalysis, I eulogize the advent of a skin-ego (D. Anzieu, 1985), covering and protecting, malleable and strong, which accompanies the subject through the inclemencies of existence. This covering, a basic imaginary psychic space, enfolds the whole body and guards it from outrages and violence. It is an epidermic skin-ego without fissures, which can be torn but can also heal itself if it were. Analytic practice shows how difficult it is to obtain this good covering for oneself and how much muscular armour will be encountered (Bick [1968], quoted by D. Anzieu in *The Skin-Ego*) or defensive virginities with an underlying damaged skin-ego (filtering skin-ego). I listen to young women who are throwing themselves into a search for an erogenous body and who reveal—under the appearance of a demand for object-relations—an injured skin-ego that desperately seeks (without being able to entrust nor to wait for the adequate object) another skin with which to recreate a common skin and calm the painful anxiety arising from the injuries of the skin-ego—those "wounds of the soul" that will not heal (see chapter two, "Giving oneself a body, sharing bodies").

Lacking an adequate skin-ego, sensuality is contaminated, scattered, and impoverished. The sense of self, this place of pure stone (see chapter two), should be a sort of sarmentum supporting the axis of the sensual happenings. The woman lost to herself will demand from sensuality what it cannot give her. It will be a sensuality that she has forced, which will sometimes be devastating, but a bitter sensuality, as though the *pleasure in oneself* were a component of enormous importance for the integration of sensuality with the object-relations of life.

Virginity injects the sacred, the sublime, into eroticism.

The virginity I am praising is self-integrity. It is the feminine figure that cannot be degraded. It knows only well-being and exerts a kind of self-eroticism of its own, a fleshless sensuality, an eroticism that is bodiless.

The impossible is made flesh in the immaculate Virgin; it is good for the fellow being, passed on to the child, transmitted outside oneself. We have here "the virgin devoid of the signs of power and of the science of the powerful" (Nobecourt-Granier, 1981). On the virgin rock of the subject, in the place of "pure stone", is built the ethical scaffolding of the subject. The humble giver of divine life lets a beam of want filter through her image.

Kristeva (1987) thinks along these lines when she writes: ". . . at the side of this ideal totality which no single woman could incarnate, the Virgin is also turned into the anchor-point of the humanization of the Occident and the humanization of love in particular."

I add finally that the virgin part of a subject is the intimate, secret part, the territory of the unconscious properly speaking, the space occupied by the famous navel of the inaccessible dream of Freudian theory. And it is also that which is waiting to be conquered, the virgin forest of our thoughts and our desires, the area that will be deflowered in exploration and discovery. Recent writers have become aware of this idea of sublimation. The poet T. S. Eliot (1944) writes: "Old men ought to be explorers." Is this not perhaps an admonition to persist in penetrating the new, that which is waiting in hiding? It is that "Light, more light" which another poet, Goethe, is said to have uttered as a farewell at the moment of his death.

Interminable virgin lands are waiting in silence for someone who is daring enough to reveal them.

Virginity as phallic armour

> . . . now he knew that virginity is a form of greed, and that the body rises again to give and take, to take and give, ungreedily.
>
> Now he knew that he had risen for the woman, the women who knew the greater life of the body, not greedy to give, not greedy to take, and with whom he could mingle his body.
>
> [D. H. Lawrence, "The Escaped Cock", p. 140]

It can be observed that, in the integrity of a body never penetrated by a man, a woman carries a sort of "invincible virginity". It constitutes, in a certain form, an aberrant destiny of the libido, as she cannot go in search of another body on which to bestow her erogeneity. Virginity acquires a phallic power that confers a special charisma on the virgin. She symbolizes "self-enjoyment", showing enjoyment as a cause in itself (Assoun, 1983), and there appears in her an attractive absolute authority. Sometimes this virginity, this ultra-celibacy, hides an unconscious fidelity to another significant person with whom she has celebrated a secret marriage.

> Thus Sara came to my consulting-rooms, 55 years old, a virgin, handsome and elegant. Her parents had died, and it was the depression resulting from this mourning that led her to come and see me. For the rest, everything was in order. She was an only child, and she paid religiously every month for the vault in the cemetery where she planned to lie after her death, in the exact place between her father and her mother. She kept her body chaste, unconsciously giving herself to the loves of her whole life (father and mother), between whom she lived in phantasy, and with whom she felt intimately united in the life beyond. This "little girl" laughed and blushed at the slightest reference to her erogenous body; according to her, it did not exist. She had never felt erogenous sensations, she had never masturbated. Intact in her body, penetrated psychically by eternal vows to her primal objects, Sara was proud of her virginity. She enjoyed the idea of knowing herself uncontaminated by sexual contacts, which she considered repugnant. One day, referring to the genitals of a man she knew, she smiled

mischievously, leaning towards hysteria, imagining the testicles hanging limply because of the age of the man. At most, her erogeneity is expressed in the fact of sleeping in the same bed as had her dead father—incest at a distance, without guilt or punishment, and "without sex nor death" as Kristeva (1987) writes about the virgin. Sara does not have to die: she will simply slip from her father's bed to the closeness of the niche. She is for ever in eternal good company, both on earth and beyond.

The erogenous body is scarcely insinuated. Saint John Chrysostom (quoted by Kristeva) writes: "where there is death there is also sexual copulation"; in Sara virginity functions as a fetish and as a protective phallic emblem.

The intact hymen acquires a defensive quality. In mythology the hymen is the battle armour of the goddess Pallas Athene, the combatant virgin in whose honour women fight in contests. The Sauromatas—according to Hippocrates—"make war while they are virgins; they do not marry without first having killed three enemies and they do not live with their husbands before they have carried out the sacrifices prescribed by law" ("of airs, waters, places", quoted by Huston). The Amazons, too, are women bearing arms, virgin warriors rather than women, fierce virgins who have not capitulated to the weakness of the flesh and who maintain their strength through an intact vagina, which gives their bodies a guarantee of power. The state of virginity demolishes the man's ancestral right of propriety over the woman; the man cannot make a woman "his"—she claims that she belongs to herself. The conforming equations are: hymen–private psychic space–protected intimacy–combative power.

Of the fear of defloration and of interminable defloration

The hymen marks the limit between an unknown interior and the perceptible exterior. It is the entrance door to another bodily territory, invisible but palpable, rich in erogenous resonances and dangerous at the same time. To break that hymen is part of the "primal act" (Freud, 1918a), simultaneously feared and desired.

Rereading Freud's text "The Taboo of Virginity" (1918a) is always stimulating and gives rise to many reflections. He speaks of "a fear fundamental to the woman"—as though the woman, or "womanness", were something that is on guard inside the body. In the penetration of her body the greatest dangers are those brought by pain . . . and blood. These two elements mixed with erotic desire are enough to bring about the sensation of the sinister. Perhaps that is why Freud, when he says that the woman is very different from the man, describes her as incomprehensible, enigmatic, singular, and above all, inimical. I quote a short sentence by Freud: "The man is afraid of being weakened by the woman, infected with her femininity, and of then showing himself incapable." Inside a woman lies a mystery that can weaken men. It is not only the struggle between the sexes that is involved, but also the difference between the sexes and its psychic consequences. Blood–pain–castration–death are equations that impose themselves, and the human being wants to know little of that. The woman herself often starts to struggle against herself because she fears becoming infected by her own femininity and entering on the affective sensorial paths of her growing erogenization. To the phantasy of "weakening", of "putting oneself at the mercy of", is added a vengeful fury against man, who is supposedly powerful and dominating (see chapter three).

Freud (1918a) is almost amusing when he relates how a woman insulted and struck her husband after every satisfactory coitus. In the hostility at the time of surrender is shown ambivalence and the need to reconfirm that her identity has not been diminished. The struggle and the insult represent an act of self-affirmation, of reorganization of her limits and recomposition of her individuality. Above all, she must bear in mind the effect of the early anxieties about her body that may be reactivated during the erogenous contact when it is robbed, destroyed, violated. Melanie Klein (1975) has made important contributions on this subject.

The frequent occurrence of frigidity in the woman at the first coitus suggests an elemental condition in which feminine sensuality is involved: it is the category of the gradual, of always "more" in the universe of sensations that are awakened in her. Biologically deflowered, a woman may remain dormant in her erogenous–affective–sensorial potentiality. She then maintains a latent virginity.

When, therefore, I refer to "virginities" (and I emphasize the plural), I want to point out that I am speaking of a body that transcends anatomical and physiological limits, in which is written the history of parental desires, of phantasies, and that is in its turn the field in which there unfolds an unconscious language in close relationship with something that cannot be represented or formulated.

The variety in the quality and quantity of the waves of voluptuousness that a feminine woman is capable of unfolding requires successive explorations and bodily adventures through which the woman "opens her flesh", cancels the repression of her affective body, surrenders to her senses, and raises the level of her orgasmic capacity.

Defloration has no final point. The virginity of one's fellow being surrounds it with interest and invites one to explore it intimately. Interminable virginity may make a subject infinitely loved and attractive to another.

In an interesting work, Marie Langer (1949) analyses a novel by Jules Verne. She shows how events in the internal world in his narrative relate to defloration. The novel refers to the deflowering of the earth-mother and to the fears awakened by overcoming the resistance of the hymen and reaching the bottom of a volcano–tunnel. There waits the revelation of the mystery of life and death. Langer (1951) affirms that man compares the hymen with an illusory penis at the moment of defloration. I think it is a question of avoiding the consciousness of the void, the painful recognition of "not being", "not having". Once again, nothingness.

Virginity can similarly be partial (one part of the body must remain untouchable, one orifice must never be penetrated). Various taboos accompany the various virginities that are now no longer localized in the hymen and the vaginal cavity. The concept of virginity extends to every sensual avoidance: now the breasts will be avoided in caresses, now there is a certain contact, now the time to make love will be stipulated, now the position in which the bodies are intertwined, and so on.

Refloration

Defloration and refloration are alternating concepts. To regain virginity means to regain in oneself the state of intactness after a break has taken place in one's covering. To return to being a virgin at a psychic level implies recovering the integrity lost in successive penetrations or adventures of life. In a sort of psychic rebirth, magnificently virgin once more, the woman recreates pseudo-bodily coverings. Living is penetrating, violating, forcing, for which there may be brought into play now the knowing instinct in sublimations, now the contrectation instinct in going towards new object-relations, now the sex-instinct in bonds of love, and so on. The novel is found, difference is discovered, a state of openness takes place. Then, with the recovery of the state of closedness, refloration is established.

In love-life, widowhood, the departure of a beloved person, or forced or voluntary abstinence create situations that re-establish virginity. The "first time" becomes possible again. From anthropology Freud (1918a) tells of widows who had to be deflowered again and recover the danger inherent in the virgin. He refers to Schnitzler's short story, *The Fate of Freiherr von Leisenbogh,* in which "the lover of an actress who is very experienced in love is dying as the result of an accident. He creates a *new virginity* for her by putting a curse of death on the man who is the first to possess her after himself" (p. 207n; italics added).

A hymen with many layers: Eva's dreams

The dream of a young analysand, near the date of her marriage, may serve to illustrate what I have just explained.

> This was a dream between two consecutive sessions. At the first session Eva was irritable and suffered from a symptom that had appeared recently: tachycardia. The doctor had examined her and found her to be well. Her illness was certainly of a psychosomatic nature and part of the actual neurosis.

Her fiancé, in their love-life, "is always considerate, always thinks of me, he does not only think of his pleasure".

But the tachycardia persisted, and the dream furnished an important key, together with the disappearance of the symptom.

The dream was as follows:

"I went to the doctor to consult him about the tachycardia, and what he said to me was that what was happening to me had to do with the fact that I was a virgin. 'In spite of everything, organically you are still a virgin.' How can that be? I asked him. I did not understand the connection ... suddenly he was not my doctor, he was a young woman two or three years older than me, she was waiting for me in my mother's bathroom, she was sitting in the bath. 'Yes—she said—as you are going to get married.' As though the hymen had various layers, and not all of them had been broken. ... In another moment I was with Esteban (her fiancé), *and I could not sit down beside him ... how could it be that I was still a virgin? I thought angrily how complicated sexuality was."*

In associations she said she felt shame about speaking of such things, "as I am not all that good in bed, I'm aware of my inhibitions ... I'm letting him think it is so, and I know it is not so."

The unconscious desire of the dream can manifestly relate to a desire to marry as a virgin, according to religious custom. On the other hand, she associates virginity with excitement and with the eczema from which she suffers in certain circumstances. She associates the hymen with the diaphragm and its difficulties and her repugnance at putting it in and taking it out. It irritates her to touch her genitals. In the same way, her doctor's medical examination panics her. This "opening her legs" to another woman opens the inter-woman dimension. She is a woman's virgin, a virgin of herself, as though the coverings on her body were metaphors for the coverings on her psyche. She associates coverings with tissues and with a documentary on the customs of certain Indians, which she happened to see on television. She says:

"At the first menstruation they were doing drawings on the girl with spines, it disgusted me so much that I covered my eyes . . . then they did a dance to choose a warrior to deflower her . . . virgins had to bear that . . . it made such an impression on me . . . how sometimes they got infected . . . to damage the body was a pride . . . they were scarred for life. . . . I was disgusted to see it with all the blood . . . bruises . . . discharges."

In this analysand blood, virginity, pain, disgust, and humiliating submission to the man, with the consequent hostility, are closely associated. She is perturbed by the imminence of "sharing the bed", of that "bed for two" which she is soon to occupy. She, who has concerned herself with adequately guiding her future husband in his passionate effusions, fears the nearness that would lead her to new deflorations. The analysis of this dream allowed me to become aware that certain caresses are forbidden to the fiancé, and there are prohibited zones and love-play (partial virginities). Sometimes she hastily draws back her hand from the warm contact of her partner's hand. She stiffens it (imaginary hand–phallus) and in this way avoids the waves of voluptuousness and the perturbation of sensual stimulus.

The tachycardia is a somatic manifestation of the anxious waiting (Freud, 1984a) for "something" to happen in her erogenous body. This "something" is associated with homosexual anal contents with the mother, the first body of love (scene in the bath).

Another dream, with more threatening nuances, followed this one: *A man is pursuing her. She runs into a house. There are many doors. The man breaks them down one after another in search of his prey. He is going to rape her. She runs in terror. Finally the climate changes: the bad man is now her fiancé, who protects her.* The house symbolizes her body. The doors symbolize her virginities. Eva fears the masculine virile force that she envies enormously. The man, shattering the interior of her body and breaking her defence-doors time and again, expresses the unconscious desire for "more, always more"—the wish to be deflowered intensely, "door by door". The dream also expresses the desire to have at her side a rough and sweetly protective man, a combination that must help her to pass the obstacles of her phallic nature and reach feminine sensual pleasure.

Virginity of enjoyment, virginity of pleasure, virginity of sensual liberties

The following clinical vignette is a good illustration of my idea.

Virginia

Virginia had been married for some years. Her erogenous exercises with her husband were limited and controlled. She did not allow him to ejaculate in her vagina (they have chosen this method of contraception), and she bestowed indulgence and caresses only grudgingly. Some time later she took a lover—a friend of her father's. Recounting in the session the quarrel with her husband during which she declared her conjugal infidelity, she uttered the following words: "I told him that I was trying to make a new life. I told him that I had discovered that I was a woman, and at his side I would have died a virgin."

Virginia had been deflowered by two men. The first was her husband, who performed the first act of perforating the hymen. He thus received both the pre-oedipal hate for the mother-object (Freud, 1914c, 1931b) and the hate for whoever dared to penetrate and weaken her feminine flesh, and make it bleed and hurt. She punished him incessantly by rejection, the lack of all sensual pleasure, and the manifestations of disgust and repugnance, the fruit of the barriers of censure. The second to deflower her was the father–lover. Sustained by transgression in the path of incestuous phantasy, Virginia managed to turn loose the repression of the libido and knew pleasures derived from liberties of her senses.

Simone de Beauvoir (1987, p. 119) says that the Romans called Messalina "unconquered" because none of her lovers had given her pleasure. We can see that the "virgin of pleasure" concept was already present in antiquity.

CHAPTER FIVE

The dissolution [*Untergang*] of the Oedipus complex in women

Introduction

Before going into this theme in greater depth I want to look at the German term *Untergang*, which Freud uses to designate what the English translation calls "dissolution". In French the term "decline" [*déclin*] is used. The German word is used in connection with a boat, a ship, or a person who is sinking. Literally, it means "going down" [*unter:* down, and *gang* from *gehen:* to go]. It is also used to designate sunset (when the sun goes down). The connotation I am trying to bring out is that of a *slow* sinking, which accords with the word "decline".

The combination of these words in the attempt to translate the dissolution of the Oedipus complex brings us near to the true sense of the term *Untergang*.[1]

From the beginning the Oedipus complex represented a crucial idea in psychoanalysis, a psychic space where phantasies, identifications, and libidinal desires meet. It indicates a psychic time with a regulating character. The dissolution of the Oedipus complex precipitates a sediment that is the results of the completed psychic work.

According to Freud (1925j), "in girls the motive for the demolition of the Oedipus complex is lacking" (p. 257). He insists repeatedly (1924d) in this context: "... our insight into these developmental processes in girls is unsatisfactory, incomplete and vague" (p. 179).

I part from Freudian theory on this point, and in this book I suggest the ending of the Oedipus complex in the woman. This outcome can be spontaneously observed in many women. In others it is liquidated through repression. Psychopathology, with its wide-ranging ideas, can teach us a great deal about false resolutions and distortions of the Oedipus complex.

To make this clearer, I have to describe four phases in woman's life. I shall linger especially over the last, in which my tests of decline come into play. I shall also take care to bring out, together with modifications in psychism, the correlates at the level of the erogenization of the body. In the last part I illustrate what I have said with clinical material.

The first phases

There exists a first phase, which Aulagnier (1975) describes with clarity and which occurs when the infant faces for the first time the penetrating violence of maternal desire, that impresses the first significant marks on its flesh. At this time of passivity the baby will be enjoyed. From the Other comes this first invading, fragmenting enjoyment, present from the first experiences of satisfaction and pain. The new little being is at the mercy of the Other, which brings it the code and sustains it in its primordial helplessness. With this first contact it interacts with the mother's body and with the productions of the maternal psyche. In the first bodily interchanges between mother and child there occurs what Freud (1905c) calls "a sort of orgasm", referring to the post-suckling state of plethoric surrender and beatitude.

This moment can be categorized as one of *primordial femininity.* Boys and girls experience this first enjoyment as it applies to them: being loved, cared for, supported. It is a feminine passive position rich in erogeneity, in which the first intersubjective interweaving takes place. Vulnerability, defencelessness, that "anxiogenic beginning of existing in the world", extreme dependency, are all factors that help us to understand the general "rejection of femininity" both in men and in women. Freud locates this rejection in the living rock of castration (1937c).

The second phase diminishes the fragility of the first time. It is of the time of phallic enjoyment (Lacan). The girl or boy fills the mother to the brim, constituting a double completeness. The body, representing an imaginary phallus, closes a crevice of want over the maternal body. It is a time of activity, of possession. The child plays at being the phallus, and the difference of the sexes does not interfere with the possibility of erogenizing the whole body. Castration is evaded. This imaginary primal phallic value remains attached to an intensely cathected mother–woman's body. At the bodily level it inaugurates what I call "the preferred form", thus indicating that the first erotic matrix takes place in the desirous interchange with the sweet body of a woman. Human flesh is narcissized and loved, before the difference of the sexes enters its complex of conflicts.

In the third phase—that of sexual difference—the paths of girl and boy diverge. It is the time of penis envy and the sadness of having been born a woman.

The phallic value is ascribed to the penis–phallus. It is the time of the first questions: Why have I no penis? Where do babies come from? are fundamental questions (Freud, 1908c, 1925j). Both sexes show their curiosity about the vicissitudes of the anatomy and the results of the difference.

The mechanism of denial pertains to this phase: "Everyone has a penis" helps the little girl to tolerate her anxiety when facing the traumatic perception of her imaginary lack. The girl puts her clitoris in the category of penis–phallus in an attempt to belong to the esteemed class. The desirous illusion of soon seeing a penis grow in the place of her genitals grows into the realization of the fallacious character of denial. Not only has she no penis, but she is not going to grow one, or else it has been cut off as some imaginary punishment. One sign fewer is traced on her body. The good anatomical form of that outstanding organ, so greatly valued and loaded with anatomical, libidinal, and phantasmatic factors (Nasio, 1989), is forbidden to her. It is a disgrace of the anatomy, an apparent biological tragedy for the being that has been born a woman.

Here the erogenous idylls break off. The imaginary absence comes to the fore. Freud described this period in detail (1931b, 1933a), citing disillusion of the mother, wounded narcissism, and entry into the Oedipus situation, where the girl imagines that she is castrated. It is the time of change of object (from the mother to the father), and hate, narcissistic fury, are useful in so far as they facilitate this necessary step. It is a time of rivalry, of resignation, and of hope (one day she will have her father's child, the child of a man in compensation for what she lacks). There is both a depressive equation—I have no penis = I have no phallus—and a revindicative equation—phallus = penis—with which the young girl flourishes an imaginary penis–phallus that destroys any penis–phallus that may interpose itself. It is the equation of the complex of masculinity. The "between women"—that intersubjective space which opens in the interchange of women—is tinged with envious rivalry and shared sadness. They will make jealous comparisons among themselves to detect who received it from the mother or the father.

Joan Riviere (1927) enriched this problem by describing how the woman will don a mask of femininity to drive away the phantasies of retaliation for having dared to exercise her possession of a phallus.

The erogenous body suffers. Freud (1940a [1938]) points out that the little girl often stops masturbating because she cannot bear contact with an imaginary mutilated anatomy. The enjoyment is precise, in the masculine way, and it materializes—concentrated in a single organ—in the clitoris–penis. The diffusion of eroticism proper to the feminine is lost. The body may contrive to anaesthetize itself to the phallic conflict, and in this case "waves of repression" come upon it. They may become frigid, or freeze (frigid–cold). Others, who are luckier, will resign themselves and remain in the Oedipus complex, as Freud postulated.

Decline of the Oedipus complex in the woman

I differ from Freud's theory on this point. My idea is that women undergo a wrecking of the Oedipus complex, at a time that must be seen as one of affirmation.

When this decline starts—as I shall tentatively illustrate with clinical material—a new sort of "somato-psychical act" takes place. Not only does the revindication of the penis–phallus cease, but the meeting with the positivization of "not having" becomes a new category. On a phallic order that covers the lack is now superimposed a non-phallic order, a feminine order, established in the lack and transmitting the acceptance of castration, the mystery of the unknown, the perishable. This movement would consist of two phases: first, it would imply accepting castration and the narcissistic blow of "not having", and, second, beyond the penis–phallus, reaching the plateau of "not having", affirming oneself there, and simply "being" a woman. This finding modifies the structure of the feminine woman's ego. Even if it is outside the limits of this book, it is still important to consider these modifications in the ego, where a probable transformation of the essential narcissism enables the body to distance itself from ideas about the penis and phallus and to reach a certain degree of working through of castration.

Negation does not directly affect the object considered: that is, "not having a penis" tells us nothing about what the woman does have. The phase of affirmation reveals new equations of having. The signifiers flow: complete Void, potential life, virtuality, mystery. . . . Void written with a capital letter acquires "full quality, consistency, truth" (Laporte, 1975). These new equations or commutative series mark a "more still" in the exercise of femininity.

At this stage there is no change of object. There is a delaying over oneself—that is to say taking oneself as object in a sort of intrapsychic redoubling, which generates a narcissistic re-flow on the ego.

The changes that take place in the ego bring with them a modification in object-relations: less dependence, greater self-affirmation, greater capacity for being alone. The woman's self-esteem gains strength. At this stage of affirmation the adventure begins of inhabiting one's own psychic space, placing oneself "well in one's skin". It is the time of saying farewell to alienating identifications with primal objects and transient inhibitions in object-choice. As a work of disidentification of primal objects has been completed, later choices can be made within a more ample exogamizing spectrum.

The affirmation stage includes a moment of trophic solitude. The woman is engaged in tranquil waiting, which presupposes that she has gained a feeling of basic confidence.

At this stage of affirmation and accompanying inhibition in object-choice, the intrapsychic unfolding derives from what I have called "intrapsychic maternalization". This is an intrasubjective movement, through which the subject takes herself as object of support, care, and love. This element of maternalization does not come from the penis–child equation or from penis-envy, but from love of oneself projected in a second period onto the objects of the external world: companion, child, and so on. Intrapsychic maternalization will have to be followed by the desire to be a mother to the loved one. (Does Freud not perhaps say that of fundamental importance for the success of a marriage is the fact that the woman can see her companion in part as a son?) Trophic narcissization emptied out on the ego in the period of affirmation will allow it to be projected later onto objects of the external world.

When the Oedipus situation is resolved without much conflict, this phase passes almost unnoticed. However, the same does not happen in clinical material on neuroses, in which it occupies a fundamental and decisive structural space, before the decline of the Oedipus complex.

The positive intrasubjectivity of being at peace with oneself expands in the interchange with other women in a sublimated homosexual bond, free from phallic rivalry. Then a fertile "between-women" zone opens, in which women, as Xaviere Gauthier (n.d.) says, "dance, live, enjoy". This "between-women" is similarly a good prelude to bodily erogenization. "Between them" they transmit the alchemical secret of feminine enjoyment, which later they will have to expand in desirous interchanges with men.

A structural potentiality emerges when the penis–phallus distance is gained. The phallus stops being exclusively a masculine attribute. Through the metaphorical–metonymic displacements the woman can attach herself freely to the phallic values that are essential for her exogamic trajectory. She gains bisexuality, with all its richness. On the one hand, she now knows that phallicism is not forbidden to her; on the other, beyond the phallus, she recovers her primordial femininity, leaps the defensive wall of penis envy, and surrenders to an "active passivity" in a delicious self-affirmation of her self-esteem. This movement of affirmation allows her, in her femininity, to "break free from the penis" as a phallic attribute and to fling herself into an intrapsychic adventure in her internal world and in her erogenous body.

Instead of sadness and rivalry, she will have tranquillity and joy.

Bela Grunberger (1973) and Janine Chasseguet-Smirgel (1964), among other authors, brought out the importance of intersubjective dependence in the life of a woman, her need for narcissistic confirmation and her precariousness as regards finding sufficient self-esteem in herself. Now, with the decline of the Oedipus complex and the accompanying transformation of her narcissism (Alizade, 1987b), the woman has gained access to greater internal freedom. Feminine enjoyment—that excessive enjoyment which Lacan describes—tells of the "more" in her erogenous body; the joy that comes to meet her tells of the "more" in her psychic life.

The erogenous richness I have described on earlier occasions (Alizade, 1988b, 1989) now unfolds. The vagina, the clitoris, the anus, the breasts, the mouth, the whole body, in short, coalesces in a diffusion of feminine eroticism, which takes the woman back to the first times of joyous erogenous effusions.

The different times or movements described in these pages are intermingled and, like "streams of lava", rush down, one on top of the other. It is necessary that that "something" of every woman reaches this movement of affirmation. Thus she can aspire to be a true partner to the man, both recognized in the truth of symbolic castration, which blurs the difference between the sexes and inexorably forces us to face the living boundary of our needs, imaginary mirages having been overcome.

Clinical material

Nora

Nora is a beautiful young girl. Born after several male siblings and the daughter of a successful father who is "always in command", she tends to be gloomy and irritable, seeing her fiancé as a rival and often quarrelling with him.

She came into the world as a substitute for a male child who had died a few days after birth. While pregnant with Nora, her mother lost her own mother. As she tells it, in photos in the family album the mother, dressed in deep mourning, and with a distant expression on her face, is holding her, a new-born baby, in her arms. Years later she would tell Nora that with so much mourning she "couldn't stand her".

These early upsets in the intersubjective relationship left their mark. To the process of deficient trophic narcissization, which obstructed the plenitude of phallic enjoyment in the conquest of the mother's love (she could not complete it), is added a devastating exaggerated anxiety, which probably led her to seek refuge in early phallicism and a certain rejection of femininity.

Thus she talks of her limited, controlled erogeneity, of her fear of surrender in amorous interchanges, of her own difficulty in "feeling".

> Returning from a time spent skiing, she says: "I always put myself in that position, striving to beat the man, and end up fighting. . . . I was one of those who skied best, I made efforts to come out best, I was afraid to look too important [*capa*], I could not stay behind."

"Capa" was a signifier that was transferred from important to *capada* [castrated], without, insignificant, unimportant.

It was through a series of successive dreams that a structural crystallization began to be perceived, after several years of analytic work. These dreams presaged the change from the stage of penis–phallus envy to that of the affirmation of femininity delineated earlier.

First dream: woman's body

"I dreamed of floods of water, dirty water; I was clinging to a post in a corner, I had a ball in my hand, I had to swim against the current, the water disgusted me, there might have been rats in it, I was swimming the crawl and I couldn't, I had to swim breast-stroke, I had to grasp the post again, my fiancé came and caught me by the arm, I raised myself with disgust, all the filth that could pass between my legs was passing, it gave me nausea, my fiancé gave me protection."

Through the associations the rats and disgust drifted into shit–scabs–whores–dirt, going through unknown places. The displacement that took place was rat–penis–disgust—disgust that she associates with seedy hotels to which couples resort. The crotch brings a reference to shit–blood–discharge–disgust once more.

"Swimming against the current" could indicate the installation of the erogenous movement of regression and the attempt to approach repressed bodily representations.

The masculine (fiancé, the post to which she clings) alludes to a secure penis–phallus. The feminine emerges as a place of rejection, a fluid and changing place in the body, a space of strong current (going over dangerous ski-slopes—breaking loose from the post—facing the current—feeling between the legs). The dream also speaks of a change of style (swimming breaststroke).

Second dream:
of the ladder for a single foot, the long skirt, and the fall

"I dreamed I was going into an old building with my cousin and my aunt, and there was a ladder that I could get only one foot onto, I could not go up that way, I was wearing a long skirt, it got caught and tangled and annoyed me. I managed to go up, but I could not raise my leg over the railing, and I found myself hanging in the void by a chain, and I saw that other people were going up the normal ladder and arriving at the same place. I threw myself into the void to catch the ladder, and I was angry. I went through the street, I was wearing a beige skirt, a grey jacket, and a black sweater, all big. I thought: what am I dressed like! I have to go away quickly and start studying."

"Long skirt" stands out among her associations; she associates it with an episode: "the other day I was standing at the corner of the building with a new skirt; a girl went past and said to me: 'What a pretty skirt!' The girl was pregnant." Then she associates it with a bridal gown. (These associations support the observations of Garma (1949) about the symbolism of clothes in dreams.) Nora, in the dream, got free of the chain and flung herself into a new adventure. The obsessive defences (starting to study) appear together with a certain estrangement from herself (new big clothes). "To start studying" is associated with knowledge of a different order. "Big" was associated with a body that swells in pregnancy, and also with importance.

Third dream: of women playing happily with their heads down

"Last night I dreamed that we were in a box at the theatre. We were turning round and we remained with our heads down, and a tall lady did not turn round, I wanted to put my legs into a pipe so as not to fall over, I could not bear the feeling, I saw Lucia and other friends, they were laughing, 'Come and see how nice it is.' They were very free, hanging over, and I was clinging to the pipe and didn't move away."

Lucia is a friend "with a good mother, always in a good mood, joyful, ready for anything". She seems to represent a feminine ideal in which bisexuality is harmoniously integrated. She admires her, works, speaks languages, dances. Nora finds herself in a happy scene in which women laugh and amuse themselves.

This scene contrasts with a vivid real one two years earlier: "Various friends are playing in the garden, they are falling on the grass one on top of the other, there is sun and laughter. I move away and go to the kitchen. There, from behind the window-pane, I watch them playing."

A few sessions earlier, Nora had announced the changes she was experiencing: "I see myself more liberated from things, . . . as though I had entered into another zone."

The working-through of these dreams and later material enabled me to study in detail in the peculiarities of this patient the development of the time of affirmation and the gradual resolution of her Oedipus complex.

Syntheses and conclusions

I leave these lines with the feeling of having sketched an important movement in the Oedipus complex in women. Later investigations will rectify and complete the picture delineated here and will make it possible to articulate these considerations with other elements of the theoretical and clinical body of psychoanalysis.

In short, the decline of the Oedipus complex in women constitutes a "new somato-psychic act", which has as a corollary the distancing between the representation of the penis and that of the phallus (penis ≠ phallus), the assumption of bisexuality, the overcoming of the point of horror of imaginary castration, the installation of a non-phallic symbolic order or feminine order, the intensification of the affect of joy, the recovery of primal femininity, and the transformation of narcissism.

Note

1. I am grateful to Dr. Didier Anzieu for having put me on the track of this nuance of translation.

CHAPTER SIX

Faithfulness–unfaithfulness

Nous deux nous ne vivons que pour être fidèles à la vie.

Both of us live only to be faithful to life.

Paul Eluard, "Poésie ininterrompue"

When structures of faithfulness are created, they are valuable because they can shape a sense of identity, of kinship with a family, a nation, a tradition. They give psychic relief by providing criteria that are rooted in traditions that transcend the generations.

These are multidisciplinary terms that are difficult to define in the language of psychoanalysis. To talk of "faithfulness to an object" may imply a fundamental unfaithfulness to oneself, or vice versa. We can look at it either objectively or subjectively. "Faithfulness" and "unfaithfulness" can become confused at the margins of relativity. On the other hand, the object to which they are directed can be quite clear. An obvious object of erotic love or passion accrues to itself inanimate objects of a higher or lower level of abstraction, such as when we find faithfulness to a religion, an idea, an activity, and so on.

The mother–child dyad is the prototype of the link created by an ideal of faithfulness. The permanence, the constancy of the irreplaceable mother-object in being what the infant requires for survival is fundamental. A space is created that is closed, secure, objectal, fusional. The mother tacitly promises to care for and love her child and, above all, promises not to abandon it while it is helpless. *Of course she will be unfaithful to it.* Just think of the vicissitudes of the Oedipus complex and the phantasy of the primal scene, and the essential unfaithfulness of the primal object becomes obvious. *To be excluded, to suffer from unfaithfulness, is a human condition.* Any other significance will reveal at some time its incapacity to fulfil the expectations of satisfaction of a certain subject, who will have to suffer successive narcissistic blows and attacks on his self-esteem in its pre-oedipal and post-oedipal journeys. Exclusion is a category that appears when being faithful or unfaithful is taken into account. It is a movement that generates structural *Gestalten* of the psychic apparatus. *Unfaithfulness is a necessary constituent of exclusion.* The triangular formation is a game where two exclude one, or where two include a third, permanently destroying the idea of an irreversible inclusion. But psychoanalysis can provide new ways of looking at this delicate question, using the uncontradictable logic of the unconscious.

To the precious constancy of the object is opposed the complexity of a metapsychology of sensual–sexual meetings, which presents a manifest content (that erogenous body given in that precise link) and a latent content subordinated to the laws of the unconscious in which opens the world of phantasies, of internal objects, of fundamental scenes, of identificatory play. This multifaceted conceptual wealth must inevitably destroy prejudices and ideologies about "doing well" with regard to sexual life.

In analytic practice we can usually observe (as I shall illustrate at the end of this chapter) scenic matrices that are a condition of eroticism for a determined subject. By scenic matrices I mean representational–affective models in a given form, which can develop at simultaneous or successive times and which make erotic life possible for a certain individual. They imply fixations on models and internal mandates (see the observation of Nadine in this chapter).

The consolidation of a feeling of oneself, of a skin-ego enwrapping without tearing or the sedimentation of a place of pure stone, as I imagined it earlier (chapter two), are all theories illustrating how an individual can emerge from the dyad and from the Oedipus complex, having cut off a skin for himself—that is, having reached a certain individuation and autonomy. In his erotic–affective life there will be no need to struggle urgently with the demand to receive an archaic and impossible faithfulness from the primal object (total, alienating, fusional, and endogamous), but faithfulness will appear as a law and a code in the organization and regulation of human erogenous–affective interchanges.

Faithfulness is seen as carrying an ethic that the subject will be able to manipulate from the margins of his liberty for his own benefit and for the benefit of the other important people involved in the acts concerning him.

I want to emphasize the distinction between two forms of faithfulness. The first is peremptory, compulsive, anxiogenic, exclusive. It refers to the claim of the primal object (archaic faithfulness). In the second form, faithfulness is exercised plastically in a link in which the participants exercise this faithfulness in accordance with a desire mediated by ethics. This form of faithfulness is always partial. The subject will be faithful to himself, faithful to his exogamous impulses, and faithful to his love-object at the same time. Given that these faithfulnesses may be incompatible, the individual must then choose (or be chosen in the rough places of his desire) to go on alternating between faithfulness and unfaithfulness. This is because the third party—the one who is different, the one who seduces, the one who evokes events and memories with their store of remembrances and experiences—will always be present. At this point faithfulness and unfaithfulness acquire a wider sense and slip metonymically through the combination of objects, leaving mere faithfulness of the body for an object of desire or love.

Every couple needs some confidence that they have a more-or-less explicit contract of mutual protection and help, and this implies the idea of faithfulness. To be the recipient of someone's faithfulness is to be given evidence not only of being loved but, and most especially, of not being hurt within the most intimate self by the narcissism of this significant other. In faithfulness, the affect of confidence facilitates the privileged cathexis of the loved one. The field of confidence established between two people offers the possibility of leaving one's partner knowing that one occupies an important fraction in the representational network of the other who will, during one's absence, persist in the function of "being for the other". An imaginary envelope of reciprocal support creates an internal area of mutual inclusion of the one in the internal world of the other.

Confidence—the desire to be "with the other and for the other" —often transcends the unconditional demand for the exclusivity of the erogenous body. The "faithful" is articulated with the "unfaithful", and in this apparently contradictory relationship we can see the impossibility of the appropriation of one subject by another. In the best of cases, beings faithful to desire may be faithful "by desire" to caring for the delights of a link enriched in a privileged way thanks to the constant exercise of protective seduction. It is interesting to record again here that in the story of the *Odyssey* the word "faithfulness" is never used in reference to Penelope (Peyrefitte, 1977), whereas synonyms of the word "confidence" abound.

It is known that prohibition is an incentive to desire and favours the movements of transgression. What is the alchemy that is expressed when, despite living together and the time spent in each other's company, two subjects can go on wanting to meet? It may be guessed that they have found an interminable formula of prohibitions and transgressions. The idea of "falling in love", or "true love" (*echte Liebe,* as Freud wrote) has become linked inevitably with faithfulness. This mysterious affect enables us to accept a being momentarily excluded if it is for the benefit of the loved one's happiness.

The concept of the "multiple object" (Alizade, 1987a) reveals the dynamics of the idea. The couple-object brings onto the scene relations and persons belonging to the pre-oedipal and post-oedipal constellations of each of the members: father, mother, friend, nursemaid, and so on. In the other are condensed numerous projections, and various roles are represented as one comes to inherit the historical phantasies of the other's infant life. When this interweaving of projections occurs in a predominantly erotic constellation, in the context of a contract of life together, in faithfulness, the magic of the unconscious (which is infinite, inexhaustible) will illuminate both subjects.

A different faithfulness is demanded, compulsive, almost perverse in the inexorable fixity of its requirements and in the suffocating climate that it usually imposes through an incessant jealousy of the chosen object. Sado-masochism in one variant or another is not slow to ensue. This is the dark face of faithfulness, monstrous in its demands and in the vital limitations that it brings with it. The space of faithfulness is, in this case, building a phobic enclosure. The imaginary absolute possession of the object calms the separation anxiety of the primal objects. It also acts as a ceiling to one's own alienated desire. The only wish is to control the desired object, and everything demands it. This "everything" reveals idealization and omnipotence on the one hand and consequent persecution on the other. In these extreme cases of a demand for faithfulness it is easy to see how one can slip into hate by persisting in controlling the object, in the obstinate desire to dominate and subjugate one's fellow being in the name of a threatening devaluation.

This is especially true if the other moves away and explores life, letting himself be seduced by new ideas, by new psychic territories (which do not necessarily include new sexual objects)—that is, if he lets desire cast its light over the multiplicity of living things. I repeat here with Sibony (1991): "Basically you can only be faithful to someone who marries you for life and not to someone who devotes the whole of his life to you." This is because the presumed faithfulness of the object removes the phantasies of castration that exist in the idea of time and forgetfulness. The lack appears to be exorcized and borders on the phantasy of eternity. The company of the other increases the quality of erotic life and suspends in the illusion of fusion the representation of finiteness. In the idea of "always being loved", the experience is one of perpetuity, and there unfolds a feeling that the intimate world created with the significant other is infinite.

Faithfulness crosses the "lines of loss" (Sibony, 1991) and tries to capture in the solidity of confidence a magic space of well-being in which there shines the affirmative rapture of a body of love that says yes and for ever over and over again.

Faithful man, unfaithful woman, and vice versa

It is difficult to construct uniform criteria on this delicate question. Perhaps through the mere fact of belonging to a particular sex one is more likely to be faithful or unfaithful? The data of history and the discoveries of psychoanalysis contradict each other. The woman who visited Freud in his consulting-rooms at the end of the nineteenth century crystallized from her neurosis a conglomerate of psychic elements in which, as Freud says, the preponderant ones were frigidity, melancholia, a repressed body, and prohibited sensuality. Successfully repressive education (Freud expressly mentions this ingredient of a woman's sexual life at that time) had brought her to accept the necessary servitude (Freud, 1918a) for good functioning in the social roles, as adjudged by society. The woman is not only faithful, she is also repressed. Plunged in the vapours of melancholia, she will weep for the loss of her libido.

In the man, on the other hand, Freud points out the dissociation of erotic life (1910a). Sexual licentiousness is complete in light, degraded women. But in the wife–mother there exists only a minimum of pleasant interchange with an eye to reproduction in an environment in which she is respected and valued. This dissociation makes unfaithfulness an almost natural state of man.

Unfaithful man–faithful woman is the usual equation.

Aulagnier (1966) thinks along the same lines. The woman will always be (the author shows this as a universal fact, independent of any social factor) a partisan of faithfulness, since "the alibi of love is indispensable for the realisation of her desire" (p. 93). Feminine narcissism intervenes at this point in bringing out a certain vulnerability, which is more inherent in the feminine being. A woman would give anything to be loved. The woman would love to return to pre-oedipal fusion, she needs to grasp a sexual object that would be dedicated to her and would compensate her in this way for her early and constant narcissistic errors, which have left indelible traces. The man, on the other hand, always—as he is impelled to, trying to drive away the phantasm of castration—has to re-affirm as a permanent conquest his state of non-castration, his condition of being a desirous subject with full autonomy of his desire. Incessant seduction can be considered, as I see it, as a sort of masculine narcissistic confirmation.

More than the adventure in itself, what interests him is to confirm again with each new erection and adventure that there is no lessening of his power, that he can give a woman enjoyment, that he can do it "nevertheless". This "nevertheless" reflects the shadow of castration projected in time. In the presumed free circulation of his desire, brought to bear on changing objects, the man will ratify his virility without feeling too much guilt, as he considers it a natural right inherent in his masculine condition. He sees the inevitable unfaithfulness as necessary to reduce the pressure of his castration anxiety. The faithful man may feel himself feminized from the social pressure that, in its turn, requires the woman to occupy a place of quietude and waiting in a time that passes.

Other texts, on the fringes of psychoanalysis (Michelet, 1859; Moreau, 1991; Panoff, 1984) bring out the essential animality of woman, her natural promiscuity. "The woman is a sinner by nature" (Guerra, 1971, quoted by Panoff, 1984). The female, nymphomaniac and adulteress, must be tamed. Strict educational means have to be applied to her. Both marriage and the convent serve as an enclosure for her. Feminine unfaithfulness is said to be written in the genes: it is inevitable, given her hereditary constitution. The woman falls easily and must be married to control her potential instinctual licentiousness.

Parent-Auber, of the Faculty of Medicine in Paris, surgeon, professor of obstetrics, and president of the Medical Hermeneutic Society, writes about the untamed woman (*L'almanach des mystères de l'amour conjugal et de l'hygiène du mariage,* 1851, quoted by Moreau, 1991):

> She goes off in a fury and seeks pleasure from the first man she comes across: she is rejected, becomes angry, threatens and perpetrates the most violent excesses. Soon her reason is clouded, her mind goes adrift, and shows all the characteristic

> symptoms of mania. Blindly moved to the carrying out of furious acts, she hits, bites and smashes with a kind of sanguinary ferocity everything which forms an obstacle to the satisfaction of her desires.

Faced with the unleashing of so much libido, violation and prostitution are converted into therapeutic alternatives. In the article "Continence" (*Dictionary of Medical Science,* 1858, quoted by Moreau, 1991), Dr. Esquirol, a specialist in the nervous diseases of women, quotes the case of a young girl from a good family who was treated without success by conventional methods.

> "One night, in a corner of a district of Paris, to the question: 'What are you doing here?' she replied: 'I am curing myself'. In fact, after ten months of accomplishing her vile work and after having had two abortions, she recovered completely, free of her self-reproaches."

Michelet tells of similar situations in the same period in his book, *Woman* (1860). The married woman seeks from her confinement to give free rein to her instincts with any sexual object that she can have within her reach: her husband's intimates, her relatives, even if they are children, and often it will be her son-in-law who enjoys her favours. The young mother-in-law, seducing her son-in-law, will take advantage simultaneously of her conquest and of the chance to keep a close eye on the new couple.

Psychoanalysis, emphasizing the notion of bisexuality and the concepts of feminine position and masculine position—or, as Winnicott wrote (1966) "separate masculine and feminine elements which are found in men and women"—cannot assert that faithfulness corresponds to women and unfaithfulness to men. In fact, psychoanalysis today repeats this affirmation, and in analytical practice many variants can be found in both men and women.

Faithfulness–unfaithfulness emerge as terms that are not only opposed, but also form logical changing shapes (sometimes of intersection, sometimes of exclusion), in accordance with the vicissitudes of one particular situation and with the metapsychological combinations that decide in a given individual on what topics and to what object he has to be faithful or unfaithful. Once more, ethics will be involved.

Some unconscious elements determining unfaithfulness

Observation of Ines

Unfaithfulness is a scene with more than two characters in which the drama of the Oedipus complex comes to life. The third party, who is excluded from the scene and whose erogenous body intervenes "in exclusion", will have to have eluded his homosexual anxieties and his oedipal situation with relative success in order to stand up to the affective–representational impact of unfaithfulness without losing too much of his self-esteem. This makes it possible for this third person to move a certain distance from the recreated primal scene and escape the passionate drama that it is capable of unleashing.

Ines was married about a year before coming to analysis. Her father had died months before her marriage. His illness had been chronic and very painful. It appeared that mourning did not occupy much place in her psychic life. Unexpectedly, at her place of work, Ines and her boss began an erotic relationship. Hidden in the work-place itself, they shut themselves in and made love in secret. Shortly afterwards, Ines invited her boss to dine at her house with her husband. That scene involving three characters was extremely pleasant. It was not long before she confessed to her husband. Hurt, he withdrew his libido from her. In this "just punishment", Ines satisfied her moral masochism.

During Ines's analysis, it was interesting to trace the intentions towards the object in reference to the unfaithfulness episode. The semantics of the act of infidelity unfolded in various directions:

1. In her action she was claiming the autonomy she desired and her right to satisfy her sexual curiosity, and not to submit to the social precept of knowing only one man sexually. She was thus establishing the equality she desired, which made it possible for her to work through her penis-envy.
2. A feature of the lover defined their relationship: his name and her father's surname were almost identical. With the lover she brought her father to life, found a vehicle for her incestuous

phantasies, and worked through her mourning. During her moments of unfaithfulness, she felt that she was enjoying the love of her father and also that she was exorcizing death.

3. The confession to the husband satisfied the need for punishment due to her unconscious death-wishes against the father, with whom she had had a very ambivalent relationship.
4. The husband took the place of the father, who was jealous when Ines went out with some boyfriend. Ines was thus repeating a memory: her father who waited up for her when she stayed out late, disobeying the order to return early. Unfaithfulness was a rebellion against the father–husband. The audacity of her unfaithfulness mobilized her narcissism, causing in time an increase in her self-esteem.

In this erogenous unfaithfulness, she was maintaining a basic faithfulness to her desire and an uncontrollable unconscious impulse to recover her primal object, her father, restoring him and letting herself be restored by him. Her unfaithfulness was an endogamous, incestuous action, which carried the unconscious aim of working through.

Faithfulness–unfaithfulness to the primal object

Observation of Nadine

Nadine's basic scene is as follows: she shared the conjugal bed with her mother (in fact it was like that up to her adolescence), and the father, for whom she says she felt indifference, slept in the next room. Immediately after, she accompanied her mother in an amorous meeting with a lover. She was excluded while they locked themselves in a room. When she went home she lied to her father, hiding the presence of the lover. It is a scene of suffering. The primal object seduced her, to be immediately unfaithful to her with a lover.

Nadine came to know her husband thanks to her mother: sitting in a confectioner's, the mother observed an attractive young man. She immediately told her young daughter to go and win him over. So Nadine married an object of her mother's desire. As soon as she was married, she relived with her husband the erotic scene on which she was fixated. She constantly supposes that he is unfaithful to her (projecting similarly on to him her own unfaithfulness to her mother when she got married). In her phantasy the mother occupies the place of the mother's lover and so she separates herself from her primal love-object.

Her unconscious guilt feelings led to a professional failure and to the impoverishment of her erotic life (she suffers from dyspareunia and lack of sexual desire). Nadine shuts herself into an archaic faithfulness at the service of a death-narcissism. Her incapacity to perpetrate the necessary unfaithfulness to the primal object condemns her to a morbid pre-oedipal bond. In her failed attempt to distinguish herself from her mother, to cut off "a skin for herself", Nadine tries to kill herself. Similarly she fears to find in transference this ensnaring primal object to which she feels herself chained for life. The phantasm of unfaithfulness projected into the husband resumes or rather starts off her despairing shriek and her agony in the face of her own incapacity to show unfaithfulness to her mother and faithfulness to herself.

CHAPTER SEVEN

On passion and passionate sensuality

Notes on passion

The word "passion" conjures up ideas of a world ruled by great and impulsive waves of emotion. "We find the term *'passion'* is originally derived from *pati,* to bear, a state of inaction: it indicates something of a passive character which is opposed to any idea of movement and an exercise of will." Thus Vincent (1986) refers to the etymology of *"passion"*. In his turn, Cournut (1977) observes that the etymology [from the Latin *pati* and the Greek *pathein*] is the same as that of "patient", "passive", and "pathetic". The *Larousse* definition is: "Violent, impetuous movement of the being towards what it desires, powerful and continuous emotion which dominates reason and directs all behaviour. Intense inclination: having a passion for gaming."

Aulagnier (1966) divides passion into four types: mystic, psychopathological, amorous, and that of knowledge. The object of passion (God, the fetish, the loved one, the object of knowledge) immediately exhibits the character of the necessary and peremptory. A sort of psychic machinery is generated, directed imperatively to establishing a constant and excessive psychic contact with the object of passion.

The only classifiable things in the list of passions are the objects at which they are aimed. They can be divided into living objects—the fruit of intense emotions (the loved or the hated person, etc.)—and inanimate objects (drugs, sport, the gods, art, science, etc.). The fact of passion, on the other hand, does not vary in its essential qualities: univocality of the object, unrestrained directionality towards it, representational–affective overflow in the context of the phantasies involving the subject–object link, underlying narcissistic vulnerability, a call to enjoyment, expectation of suffering.

The dynamics of excess combined with the experience of "being at the mercy of", involved with submission to an overwhelming force. The peremptoriness of the instinct reveals its hypertrophy as it drags any victim of passion to the verge of exaltation and frenzy. Like a runaway horse, anyone affected by passion is forced to follow a certain course, which determines him as fixed exclusively in the psychic sector, irradiated by the object of passion.

The term "passion" never defines a subject or an object, but the bond that unites them (Aulagnier, 1966). Another metapsychological categorization of passion defines it as "the overflow of the system of representations, emotions and repression" (Cournut, 1977). Uniting both approaches, passion emerges as an overflow within a link. And what is more, it is a demanding link—irremediable, incessant, excessive. No taming of the instincts is observed (Freud, 1937c); on the contrary, there is an instinctual subjugation, which effectively forces the representations and affects bound up with the scenes to come into play in the psychic bridge that has been created between the passionate subject and that longed-for object in the changes in phantasy of the fact of passion.

The quantity of representations and affects directed to the object of passion not only provokes the overflow described earlier, but it lays bare a certain anarchy between phantasy and reality, which usually causes feelings of confusion: the dimension of what is expected of that object is lost. The incoercible call of the violent force of passion in the love-impulse sometimes seems like demonic possession or a juggling of the senses.

The movement of passion is exerted sometimes symmetrically, sometimes asymmetrically. According to Aulagnier (1979), asymmetry characterizes passion. The passionate one longs for the one who receives his passion, without reciprocity. While the first suffers at not being responded to in equal measure and realizing that the object of his passion will never suffer through him, the loved one remains master of the situation, independent of it. However, in clinical practice we usually observe symmetrical situations of passion in which both protagonists feel passion for each other and against each other (when love has turned to hate). Even when one of the participants has an "excess" of passion over the other as far as the libidinal quantum is concerned, both are entrapped and subjected to the overflow and to the psychic parasitic situation that passion imposes as it absorbs the psychic energy of the subject, who is compelled to complete the work of passion—that is, to respond to the development of a time of life devoted to the service of the representations bound together in the complex of passion in question.

Passion is like an alien body that installs itself and dwells in a subject, to incite him to a gesture, an action, an excessive word, in an "outside himself" that constitutes his essence. Because of this,

> what distinguishes passion is a halo of death. Beneath this violence, to which responds the feeling of continuous violation of discontinuous individuality, begins the dominance of habit . . . only in the violation of individual isolation—at the level of death—appears this image of the loved being which has for the lover the sense of everything he is. [Bataille, 1957]

Passion is like a madness as the subject signals to the other and waits for the response that will confirm, not only reciprocity, but also that the state of passion may continue. In symmetrical passion, the subjects involved in this experience confront each other with a phantasy: that of the possible passage from symmetry to asymmetry. In this case, one would remain at the mercy of the other.

The exclusive dyad of amorous passion asks for eternity and wants to be outside time and space. Narcissistic gratification, when found, is mirrored in the primal dyadic fusion. The regressive movement revives the fusional intensity of our early times.

Thus we can understand the tenacity with which the passionate subject grasps his object and that unwaveringness that demands that "it must be that and no other". The object is not contingent on passion—it is necessary, irreplaceable, unique. It is the guarantee of the psychic survival of a subject, who not only recreates, in the frame of passion, the archaic passion with the mother, but also defines its working-through and reparation. In asymmetrical passions, the early trauma of pathological asymmetry in the mother–child link comes on to the scene, when the primal object did not respond to the amorous longing of the infant and so produced psychic suffering in it.

Amorous passion is combined at this point with helplessness [*Hilflosigkeit*]. It emerges as a temporary palliative, which masks the subject's vulnerability. The economic function of passion is shown in the attempt to free oneself from excess, expelling it towards the exterior. The internal world seeks a way out and looks for the restitution of the balance of energy and emotion—something that is difficult to obtain. Thence the desperate solicitation of the other, who becomes the depository of a promise to repair early psychic damage. The force of instinct unites libido and the instinct for self-preservation in that sort of "psychic survival" which needs both the presence of an object of passion and the movement of passion in return.

Even when fragility and primordial helplessness are hidden beneath passion, its appearance borders on the grandiose. Passion leads to an excess in superlatives and designates extreme polarities: perfection, the better or the worse, the most intense pain, extreme hate. The passionate impulse re-animates narcissism and produces in the subject feelings that appear important, transcendent. Everything trivial or anodyne has been excluded. Faced with a void of helplessness, here is the plenitude of passion. This "passion of the other" (Vincent, 1986) blocks out the frustration of mediocrity, the tedium that results from repressed libido. The movement of excess gives a reason for living in the orbit of what is valued. The psychic bridge established with the other forms a protective psychic space, a kind of strength in which the valued is accumulated, either in the fervour of reciprocity or in the painful feeling of meeting no response. All passion makes a significant mark on a life.

Passion for the other falls into three spaces (Cournut, 1977). In the first place, it seeks a body on which to deposit its unlimited demand. This is *corporal space.* The movement of passion must couple with an object that is adequate to being the depository of the phantasy in play and of the identificatory requirements.

After this we must consider *extracorporeal space*—the imaginary space *par excellence.* It occupies all the intrapsychic and extrapsychic places through which the loved one moves. It is a capricious, changing space, which includes different scenes. There passion lives, unfolds, acts, varies its setting.

The third is *temporal space:* passion is at variance with time, it seeks a time "out of time", not subject to time's vicissitudes. In any case, it accepts a here-and-now that it wants to be immovable, since it proclaims immutability and eternity. It claims a present that is intense, overflowing, inexhaustible. If passion goes too far, its overflowing expansion will border on the demonic.

In the "body-to-body" of passion, the senses catch fire, and the sensuality threshold is lowered. This offers to individuals who have embarked on this adventure an easy way of raising erotic sensitivity. The representation of the other as "everything" and the accompanying experience of fusion act as the introduction to a real sensual orgy. This can lead to an erotic convulsion (Bataille, 1957) in the grandiloquence of feelings, in a sort of megalomania of desire, of opening out into an infinity that, even though deceptive, disregards anything small. This aim constitutes the instinctual snare of passion.

Passion carries with it an admixture of death transformed into life, expressing in its noisy manifestations the antithesis of Nirvana. It shows the almost irritating exasperation of an erogenous body phantasmatically overstimulated.

Passion does not want to exist just for the moment; it wants nothing to do with transience. It is a state that desires to be perpetual, and in its absolutism and refusal to compromise ("almost", "never", "everything", "nothing", are part of its vocabulary) it seeks to maintain a deceptive illusion that puts distance between the passionate person and the feeling of desolation.

Similarly, I want to leave a space open for the idea of passion as a global, constant, durable way of being (Cournut, 1977). This concept borders on hypomania, on the constant exercise of excess to seal off possible filtrations of anxiety. From the pathological point of view, this compulsive passion or chronic state of passion attempts to ameliorate some of the suffering that derives from castration anxiety.

Passion is an inevitable ingredient of every life that is passed through in its dimension of exploration and discovery, to the extent that it constantly shows the castration–death that is often hidden in the folds of the impetuous psychic movements that are seeking to exorcize it.

The "witch" and psychoanalysis

The "witch" is unleashed passion in the frame of an incessant transgression. The objects of passion are principally two: knowledge and sensuality. Nothing seems to hold her back in her progress towards those territories. Risk, the threat of death, are her daily bread and define the climate in which she moves—a climate that is even necessary to produce the transgressive and challenging potential that defines being a witch.

The witch, in psychoanalysis, is a metaphor for the passions that boil in the unconscious, it is "that" which makes pacts with the devil, which respects no law and laughs at every established order. Hers is the image of the sorceress with her irresistible seduction, in which the beautiful is incarnated for destructive eroticism. She is the divine demon, the beautiful in the service of evil. To say "witch" is to invoke demonic potential, the overflow of desire and an obscure and dreaded power, since the "witch" part commands the instinctual force of desire with its overwhelming impetus. In the witch we approach what is beyond the forbidden, the violence that tears through the limits and calls us to the no-man's-land of transgression.

In a session of analysis, the positions of witch, exorcist, inquisitor, and "non-witch" alternate. It is easy to understand that the analyst takes the place of the witch in her pact with the devil or that of the exorcist; it is even highly promising in the course of an analysis. On the other hand, iatrogenics make their appearance in psychoanalysis when the analyst, knowingly or otherwise, turns inquisitor in the hunt for "the witch" that underlies his patient's unconscious.

Freud said that witchcraft and a certain magic entered into analytic practice. By this we understand a transgressive work during analysis that lays bare the depths of the unconscious, leading to the appearance of surprising phantasies and the emergence of horror, the terrifying, the sinister, the impossible. The witch is a mystery that attempts to circumscribe and silence with a pejorative motto; she is the incarnation of living forces that the fires cannot burn. When Freud brings up the thorny subject of the taming of the instincts and is unable to find a satisfactory solution, he calls the witches to his aid. He appeals to a "witch metapsychology" that might throw light on this *impasse* of knowledge. And he complains: "Here, as elsewhere, what our Witch reveals is neither very clear nor very detailed" (Freud, 1937c, p. 225). That is to say, the witch does not reveal her secrets, or else the nature of the knowledge she introduces cannot be formulated in the theoretical context of psychoanalysis. So there remains something of the ineffable, the indefinite, hovering over every session; there remains a "plus" freed from the magic or lack of magic in that subtle alchemy that occurs when analyst and analysand meet.

In his self-analysis, Freud planned to descend to Hell. His correspondence with Fliess abounds in notes in which the witch and the Devil appear (Letters 56 and 57, in 1950 [1892–1899]). Freud knew the *Malleus Maleficarum* perfectly; he found in its pages resonances of the struggle between forbidden desires and the punishments of the superego. The witch started Freud on his journey of exploration into the unconscious. Thus he himself categorized his famous nursemaid (Letter 70, in 1950 [1892–1899]): ". . . my first generator (of neurosis) was a woman, old and ugly but intelligent, who spoke much to me of God and Hell, and gave me a clear idea of my mental faculties." This first witch, who showed him the path of transgression, was a sort of Mother-of-Knowledge (Assoun, 1983), a wise magician who initiated him into the exploration of the unknown.

All witches practise the sexual act with the devil. It is inferred that, reinforced by an equally powerful masculine image, the witch personifies bisexuality triumphant. The devil plays the part of the father, the seducer, and the witch, with her characteristic flight, symbolizes the desire to penetrate further and further, thanks to the transgressive acquisition of forbidden knowledge that has been snatched from nature.

The witch in psychoanalysis, therefore, constitutes a figure of "condensation": she is the one who knows, the one who can; she dares, she dominates, free and challenging, she is the cruel witch, accursed in small things—"the witch of decadence" as Michelet calls her from history. The witch is the one who floods the real with truth, putting her flesh into action in a state of enigma.

It may be said that a certain "witch" function hovers or flies in the space of each session. This witch function is what provides the magic of the interpretation, it is what generates the connections "from unconscious to unconscious", that which borders on the real. But it is a function that is sometimes feared, and analyst and analysand may, in mute complicity, decide to favour the position of "non-witch"—that is, they make a certain conventionalism prevail, an "as if" of analysis for their mutual relief. The demons will not be summoned, there will be no Witches' Sabbath in the session, the experiences of analysis will be ordered in a known frame, and the interpretations will be adjusted to the logic of the preconscious.

A vignette is relevant here (A. Yañez, "El retorno de las brujas", 1991 [unpublished]). After several years of analysis, Isabel confesses to her analyst:

> "Do you know? . . . Now I can say it. . . . At the session after my first sexual relationship, while I was telling you about it, I turned round and saw you smiling in a strange and malignant way. At that moment I thought that you were the devil tempting me and putting me on the path of evil. . . . I was afraid of you . . . nevertheless I could not do anything, I went on coming to my sessions . . . but I cannot forget your face and your smile at that moment; although I tried to, it was in vain; you are good . . . it was as though one thing did not fit with the other."

In the expression "malignant smile" there emerges the sinister, the demonic repetition of obeying the desire for the primal object. Isabel shows the imaginary metonymic closeness between voluptuousness and evil. In this counterpoint is sketched the value of the crime (Bataille, 1957) and punishment of the erotic experience. Analysis as an experience is also subject to the vicissitudes of transgressive movements that take shape in the creation of the new, the different, the "never experienced".

"Saint" and "witch"

"Saint" and "witch" represent two facets of femininity. Often they let us see their areas of intersection and the more or less violent passage from one figure to another. At one pole is the idealized woman, the great Mother who comes near to the Virgin, the woman free from concupiscence. In mystic experience the woman forgets her carnal body, which lights up in faith and living spirituality. The body-image–symbol of pure love materializes in a sublime ego-ideal. Sacred eroticism becomes detached from the substance of erogeneity and is changed to a high spiritual libidinal yearning. The saint, from her mystical point of view, shows evidence of an ethereal link in which the highest attributes become present at the behest of God.

The saint is a personage of "good"; the witch, on the contrary, fluctuates permanently between good and evil. In her passionate volubility she directs the movement of passion towards various objects. The witch is "being" in a state of passion, in a movement of overflow. Sometimes the object of her passion is knowledge, while she calculates the doses and combinations of her curative ointments and potions; sometimes it is demonic religion, commanding the mad black ceremonies of Witches' Sabbaths, invoking the presence of Satan; sometimes her passion falls upon drugs, on the henbane that she absorbs through her skin to set her upon her hallucinatory long-distance flights (Harris, 1974). In the territory of the erotic, mysticism and carnality are united. The rituals of the Witches' Sabbath mingle purificatory acts with the demonstration of sexuality in all its striking nakedness. Sex takes us towards an anti-sacredness in which the dimension of response to established religion shows the vigour and the contamination, in the form of opposition, of the very thing it is trying to extirpate: religion. The relationship of man with God is transmitted through the witch–woman, the bride of the demon, the priestess of the other religion, that of the dark, of an overflow of passion, of the real. If symbolism triumphs in accepted religions, in this anti-religion it is the real that imposes itself. On its horizon shine the experiences of death, since the fires that await it are certain. The Witches' Sabbath is a homage to daring; it is the feast in the ante-chamber of certain extermination, the laugh in the midst of plague and misery.

The witch represents free, unchained instinct. It may be said that it is an incessant impulse that condenses the exercise of many instincts, always concerned with excess, whether it is directed towards the realms of healing supported by the instinct of knowledge in the direction of sublimation or towards the realms of the erotic, the sacred, and it shows mastery in the "science of lust" and the apotheosis of the senses. The intensity of sensual enjoyment attributed to her acquires a supernatural dimension idealized by phantasy and condemned because of its off-limit existence.

The witch incarnates a movement that we bear within ourselves—one that cannot be reduced to reason. It is a movement bordering on violence, which alternately terrifies and fascinates. At its roots lies undefined transgression, a challenge to the powers of watchfulness. It borders on death, dreams, the unknown, nothingness, reality, in that exercise of pure indefatigable desire. Violence brings into play erogenous pain and pleasure. The sensual overflow calls to its service the erogenous "demonic" potential. Burning sensuality spills out beyond measure.

If the saint lays aside her carnality to become pure spirit, the witch uses this carnality as a mediator in her links with the spiritual. The witch's flesh is flesh that opens, that speaks, that asks to be annihilated, shattered by torture and seared by fire. Where the saint raises the body, the witch brings it down. The saint tames her instincts, the witch loses herself in them. The saint's body is quiet, entire, and clean. The witch's body is frenzied (she flies, whirls, fornicates), open, torn, imperfect. The saint is on the side of the eternal, the witch on the side of the perishable. One denies death, the other submerges herself in it with decision. One clings to the symbolic, the other to the real. The witch's clamour shows in the space that opens the inexhaustible path of the enigmatic, it is directed towards that which is beyond human understanding. The saint's quietude encompasses the acceptance of destiny and the sublimation of carnal sensuality. For the saint, the tranquil smile, for the witch, incoherent movements, ugliness, extreme beauty, swift progress through the forbidden, and disorder, and excess.

Saint and witch are possible extremes that come into play in the feminine order of every woman.

CHAPTER EIGHT

Feminine masochism: eroticism and the human condition

Feminine masochism as Freud (1924c) conceptualized it shows controversial facets.

I shall take up this concept of feminine masochism and try to define it. My ideas are only partly based on Freud's theories. I want to look at the concept from two points of view—one clinical, from which is derived an approach to the theme of eroticism, and the other philosophical, in which feminine masochism fits into a biological metaphor underlain by a truth of the human condition which is closely linked with nothingness.

The clinical point of view

Two premises are needed:

1. Freud wrote (1905d): "No normal man lacks an addition of perverse character to the normal sexual ends, and this general-

---

This chapter was published in the issue of the review *Imago* devoted to masochism (No. 14, December 1991. Buenos Aires: Letra Viva).

ity is sufficient to suggest *the impropriety of using the term 'perversion' in a pejorative sense*" (italics added). I extend this idea to the concept of feminine masochism. In these pages we attribute to feminine masochism a trophic, positive value that is nothing to do with masochistic perversion.

2. To make my explanation clear, I consider it fundamental to stress the specificity of feminine masochism, differentiating it from other forms of masochism, although in analytic practice we observe many mixed forms. The idea of feminine masochism that I propose frees it from the connotation of prejudice about the woman's suffering and gives it an important position in the order of instincts and in human erotic life.

Freud says that masochism "comes under our observation in three forms [*Gestalten*]: as a condition imposed on sexual excitation, as an *expression of the feminine essence* and as a norm of behaviour" (Freud, 1924c, p. 161; italics added).[1] He decides to begin his study with feminine masochism, as it does not appear to present great problems. But after a while juxtapositions and important theoretical and clinical derivations arise. In the first place, it is in men that he records it, and *once again the notion of the feminine position detached from the sex of the subject taking this attitude is emphatically brought out.* Men and women have to displace themselves to one sex or the other, and "femininity" can be manifested through this masochism, which is proper to it.

From the point of view of its evolution, Freud considers feminine masochism as a ramification of the definitive sexual organization from which are derived the characteristic conditions of femininity: being castrated, being sexually possessed, giving birth. What Freud is describing is almost a biological masochism. He shows next the points of connection between the infantile and the feminine. His description becomes complicated, however, when in the midst of his rhetoric he derives from feminine masochism masochistic phantasies that refer back to his text, "A child is being beaten" (Freud, 1919e): being gagged, bound, struck, ill-treated, and even mutilated. As I understand it, the three forms of masochism overlap, and feminine masochism is included in erogenous masochism and in moral masochism, linked with a sense of perversion.

The pure feminine masochistic element is not easy to isolate. Before considering it, I shall make a few brief points about the psychic pain arising from feminine phantasies (having stolen her father's penis, being violated, dominated), into which enter the feeling of guilt and the need for punishment, which add a quota of moral masochism to love-life (Chasseguet-Smirgel, 1964). The woman's body is transformed into a mythical scenario in which scenes of violence take place from outside (penetration by the penis, respect for male force, deflowering violation) and from inside (the painful contractions of childbirth). I agree with Cosnier (1987) that in the identification that corresponds to the feminine masochism of the genital phase there occurs an identification with the mother in coitus, and that this identification is closely linked with primal erogenous masochism and the primal relationship with the mother.

The following vignette illustrates this overlapping of masochisms in a young woman:

> Mercedes tells her analyst of her childhood phantasies, which accompanied masturbation. Shut in her room, she pretended to be tied to the legs of the bed, and while she caressed her genitals she imagined the presence of a man who was beating her with a whip. She groaned then and implored him to stop the punishment. In her life she had sought to precipitate situations of disaster by bringing into play her erogenous and moral masochism. Pain appeared as a sort of fetish: it gave her the feeling of experiencing something important. The psychic pain factor was valued to a high degree. It was only when full of pain that she felt she was alive (Abadi, 1981). On the other hand, she feared the physical pain of childbirth on the occasion of her two pregnancies. It was as if the capacity to accept feminine masochism in its positive aspect was blocked, and she could only cultivate the destructive effects of masochism.

The element of purely feminine masochism that I am trying to isolate constitutes a normal component of erotic life, which includes the factor of pain (without destruction) raised to the category of one more sense. It is the pleasure of transitivity that imitates the vulnerability of the infant in its early ages (being caressed, fed, cared for, belonging to another). It is present in the mysterious pleasure of surrender. Putting oneself in the feminine position means that one is disposed biologically and psychically to regress and become consubstantial with a primal passivity, letting oneself be compelled and swept along. Masochism intervenes, showing the instinctual co-participation (*Eros* and *Thanatos*) of eroticism.

Feminine masochism, midway between the biological and the imaginary, calls to a woman's space, a feminine space, a habitat–receptacle that introduces the subject into a real or imaginary inwardness in which the wail of "the obscure" is heard, in which there is a regression to a sinister familiarity of unknown origin. "Anatomy is destiny" is transformed into "biology creates the images of a destiny", and the gentle, the passive, the fusion of surrender and depersonalization call forth a delicious pain. This pain embedded in the concept of feminine masochism adds a quantum of exaltation of the senses in honour of an enriching orgasmic expansion (Alizade, 1989). Marie Bonaparte (1952) thinks that "a homeopathic dose of masochism is necessary to accept the most erotically feminine (female) penetration".

The positive aspect of pain has been an object of study for Benno Rosenberg (quoted by Cosnier, 1987). He writes: "The state of helplessness [*Hilflosigkeit*], when it is impossible to help oneself, is an objective state, perceived as such by the observer, but which as I see it must be differentiated from subjective helplessness." Rosenberg deduces from this helplessness, which does not cease despite the hallucination of satisfaction, "*the need for primal erogenous masochism in order to bear it*" (p. 96; italics added).

Not only can pain help to bear defencelessness, it can also be cheerfully accepted (in childbirth, for example) as forming part of a process that culminates in the gift of a child (erotic pain).

Reconsidering the characteristic situations of femininity on which feminine masochism is based, I believe this is the moment to point out the paradox of the dominating violence that is involved in the situation of being penetrated. It matters little whether we are speaking of a woman's vagina or the rectum of a woman or a man. The sinister and the unknown meet. Where am I going when I penetrate another? The revolutionary capacity of the human subject to fluctuate between feminine and masculine positions (and even to become neutral as a sexual subject) and the alternation of identificatory plays make it possible for a woman to penetrate and for a man to be penetrated. Bodies simply present their anatomies: the interweaving of the imaginary, symbolic, and real registers does the rest.

Ferenczi (1924) has made important contributions in this respect. It is enough to read his little book, *Thalassa*. Eroticism becomes a fascinating field of fiction. Coitus and birth are fused. The female's submission, the male's dominating instinct, hypnotic fascination, naked violence, the battle between the sexes and the innumerable identificatory plays and movements such as the displacement of eroticism and simultaneous sensorial elements, together form a range of erogenous potentialities directed towards the same goal, the maximum aspiration of eroticism: to return to the womb, to regress to ontogeny and phylogeny, to touch the phantasmagoria of the origins of life, and even to approach the anguish of birth and archaic experiences.

The suffering that is a part of the adventure of letting oneself go towards depersonalizing regression is a suffering—to suggest an image—like death and resurrection. There comes submersion in the tumult, the transgression of the senses, the licentiousness of the flesh, the erotic convulsion that leaves bare living materiality, the pure mortal body.

Having arrived at this point, there is no difficulty in articulating the notion put forward by Lacan (1972–1973) of an excessive enjoyment, a feminine enjoyment, an enjoyment (Lacan refers to it with irony) beyond the phallus, an enjoyment limited by what cannot be decided, in which mysticism and sensuality watch the earth with a sacred eroticism, daring to fling the body into a nameless adventure (Alizade, 1988b).

Feminine enjoyment and masochism find an area of intersection. It is a delicious suffering when between regression and feelings of annihilation the entire body—sometimes a man's, sometimes a woman's—begins a journey in which, beyond the phallic emblems, one can glimpse the almost unimaginable territory of the reality of nothingness.

The philosophical point of view

Bataille (1957) writes: "Considered as a whole, life is the intense movement which is composed of reproduction and death. Life engenders ceaselessly, but only to annihilate what it engenders. The first men had from it a confused sensation" (p. 85). This "confused sensation" must have progressed. The mystery of life and death materialized in women's bellies, which swelled and from which emerged, between violence and pain, living or dead creatures, when it was not the woman who died in the midst of the marvellous and at the same time dangerous occupation of giving birth.

The feminine images of suffering (being castrated, being sexually possessed, and giving birth) are symptoms of civilization. Femininity thus cut short builds a frontier, a defensive shield, so that the human subject may hold off a basic narcissistic pain: the limit to all omnipotence, the necessary submission to the forces of nature, the acceptance of perishability.

Feminine masochism opens a natural path on which the individual will experience in his flesh an inescapable destiny governed by a law other than the one that he will have to respect, as he is defenceless. Freud chose the term "feminine masochism" *a potiori*—that is to say, on the basis of his extreme examples. The adjective "feminine" is an extreme, close to polarity, and it indicates a limit. An alien pain runs though the flesh of the feminine body, disturbed by various events: blood flows every month, deflowering hurts, childbirth is feared. In the promised pain—"You shall bear children in pain", as the Bible says—there lies a deeper pain even than the stroke of the whip or any sadistic torture: it is the pain of wounded narcissism, the knowledge of inexorable annihilation.

Feminine masochism adopts a psychic form that—because of pain and its new significance in representations in which phantasms of want come into play—makes it possible to develop a subject's capacity to transform his narcissism (Alizade, 1987b), to decentralize from himself, to perceive the relativity of existence, and to make of the knowledge of his death an effective instrument for tempering the inclemencies of life and increasing the possibility of getting the most out of it.

Feminine masochism is a link between eroticism and death. In the words of Marie Bonaparte (1952): "I say Destruction and not Death since for me the instincts of destruction, of aggression, are not identical in essence, or co-essential with that silent decline towards the inorganic of living beings, the path of death." Feminine masochism is a vehicle of death, not of destruction. It is not for nothing that the Fates are women. Feminine pain is expressed through three stereotypes: mother, lover, death. Thus the giver of life is the same as the one who sends us back to the calm of the tomb. Freud mentions this point in his work, "The Theme of the Three Caskets" (1913c):

> The Moerae were created as a result of a discovery that warned man that he too is a part of nature and therefore subject to the immutable law of death. Something in man was bound to struggle against this subjection, for it is only with extreme unwillingness that he gives up his claim to an exceptional position. Man, as we know, makes use of his imaginative activity in order to satisfy the wishes that reality does not satisfy. So his imagination rebelled against the recognition of the truth embodied in the myth of the Moerae, and constructed instead the myth derived from it, in which the Goddess of Death was replaced by the Goddess of Love and by what was equivalent to her in human shape. [p. 299]

In eroticism, life and death are confused. The human condition is incarnated. Bataille (1957) says: "Eroticism is the approval of life even to death." When Bataille points out that the decisive act is stripping oneself naked, even when we thought we were meeting pleasure and the diversion of sex, the naked body makes signs towards an unthinkable other body: it has named the corpse, the recovered inorganic element. There filters into eroticism an obscure knowledge of the aim of everything living. In the "licentiousness of living forces", the erotic movements invite one to die (to recover continuity, says Bataille) and to revive (to return to discontinuity).

Behind feminine masochism there is the pain of "not having" and "not knowing". The body screams against the pain of impossibility, of irrepresentability and the infinite. Femininity in general, and its masochistic variant in particular, are rooted in the idea of pain. Thus castration is imagined, almost realistically, and symbolizes the inevitable tragedy of the continual annihilation of matter, which is the essence of the human condition.

Note

1. Referring to feminine masochism, Freud defines it as *"ein Ausdruck des femininen Wesens"*. Strachey translated this phrase as "an expression of the feminine nature". I want to make a special point of the word *Wesen,* which can be translated not only as "nature" but also as "essence", and as "being", "soul", "creature", etc. In philosophy it is used in the first two senses.

REFERENCES AND BIBLIOGRAPHY

Abadi, M. (1981). Protomasoquismo *versus* deuteromasoquismo. *Revista de Psicoanálisis, 38* (2).

Alizade, A. M. (1983). El chiste y su escena. *Revista de Psicoanálisis, 40* (5–6).

Alizade, A. M. (1987a). "El sentimiento de odio y el divorcio." Presented at the XXVI Symposium of the Asociacion Psicoanalitica Argentina.

Alizade, A. M. (1987b). Una direccion del narcisismo. *Revista de Psicoanálisis, 44* (1).

Alizade, A. M. (1988a). Ensayo de investigacion sobre il divorcio patologico. *Revista Argentina de Psicopatologia,* 2 (5, 1991).

Alizade, A. M. (1988b). Ensayo psicoanalitico sobre el orgasmo femenino. *Revista de Psicoanálisis, 45* (2).

Alizade, A. M. (1989). El cuerpo erogeno femenino: sus tabues y sus orgasmos (presented at the Congress of Rome of the International Psychoanalytical Association, July). *Revista de Psicoanálisis, 46* (5).

Altamirano, N. (1990). *Neruda, una lectura psicoanalitica*. Peru: Esfinge.

Andreas-Salomé, L. (1899). El ser humano como mujer. In: *Voces de femineidad* (ed. Alcira Mariam Alizade). Buenos Aires.

Andreas-Salomé, L. (1916). "Anal" und "Sexual". *Imago,* 4: 249.

Anzieu, A. (1974). Emboîtements. *Nouvelle Revue de Psychanalyse, 8*: 57–71.

Anzieu, A. (1987). The hysterical envelope. In: D. Anzieu (Ed.), *Psychic Envelopes*. London: Karnac Books, 1990.

Anzieu, D. (1970). *Eléments d'une théorie de l'interprétation*. Paris: PUF.

Anzieu, D. (1974). Le Moi-Peau. *Revue Française de Psychanalyse, 9*.

Anzieu, D. (1985). *The Skin Ego*. New Haven, CT: Yale University Press.

Anzieu, D. (1987). Formal signifiers and the ego-skin. In: *Psychic Envelopes* (pp. 1–58). London: Karnac Books, 1990.

Anzieu, D. (1990). *A Skin for Thought*. London: Karnac Books.

Assoun, P. L. (1983). *Freud et la femme*. Paris: Calmann-Levy.

Aulagnier, P. (1966). Observaciones sobre la femineidad y sus avatares. In: *Il deseo y la perversión*. Buenos Aires: Sudamericana, 1984.

Aulagnier, P. (1975). *La violencia de la interpretación*. Buenos Aires: Amorrortu, 1977.

Aulagnier, P. (1979). *Los destinos del placer*. Barcelona: Petrel, 1980.

Azzeo, R. (1991). "Formation et activité du psychosomaticien." Lecture given at the First French–Argentinian Symposium of Psychosomatic Medicine (National Academy of Medicine, 26–27 July).

Badinter, E. (1980). *L'amour en plus*. Paris: Flammarion.

Barthes, R. (1984). *Fragmentos de un discorso amoroso*. Mexico: Siglo XXI.

Bataille, G. (1957). *El erotismo*. Buenos Aires: Sur, 1960.

Bérouti, R. (1977). Orgasme, grandes orgues et petites eaux. *Revue Française de Psychanalyse*. Paris: PUF.

Bick, E. (1968). The experience of the skin in early object relations. *International Journal of Psycho-Analysis, 49*: 484–486.

Bleger, J.(1967). *Simbiosis y ambigüedad*. Buenos Aires: Paidos.

Blum, H. (1977). *Female Psychology: Contemporary Psychoanalytic Views*. New York: International Universities Press.

Bodni, O. (1991). *Psicopatologia general*. Buenos Aires: Psicoteca.

Bonaparte, M. (1949). *Female Sexuality*. London: Imago, 1953.

Bonaparte, M. (1952). Réflexions biopsychiques sur le sadomasochisme. In: *Chronos, Eros, Thanatos*. Paris: PUF; London: Imago.

Bowlby, J. (1969). *The Making and Breaking of Affectional Bonds*. London: Routledge, 1979.

Bowlby, J. (1980). *Attachment and Loss. Vol. 3*. London: Hogarth Press.

Cachard, C. (1981). Enveloppes de corps, membranes de rêves. *L'Evolution Psychiatrique, 46* (4): 847–856.

Chambon, J. (1977). Orgasme et fantasme. *Revue Française de Psychanalyse*. Paris: PUF.

Chasseguet-Smirgel, J. (1964). Female culpability. In: *Female Sexuality*. Ann Arbor, MI: University of Michigan Press, 1970. [Reprinted London: Karnac Books, 1989.]

Chasseguet-Smirgel, J. (1970). *Female Sexuality*. Ann Arbor, MI: University of Michigan Press. [Reprinted London: Karnac Books, 1989.]

Cosnier, J. (1987). Le masochisme feminin. In: *Destins de la féminité*. Paris: PUF.

Cournut, J. (1977). El orgasmo infinito. In: A. M. Alizade (Ed.), *Voces de femineidad*. Buenos Aires: 1991.

de Beauvoir, Simone (1949). *The Second Sex*. London: Pan-Macmillan, 1988.

Desroches-Noblecourt, C. (1986). *La femme au temps des pharaons*. Paris: Stock.

Dolto, F. (1982). *Sexualité féminine*. Paris: Scarabee et Compagnie.

Dolto, F.(1984). *La imagen Inconsciente del cuerpo*. Barcelona: Paidós Iberica.

Dorey, R. (1983). Introduction: Penser la transgression. In: *L'interdit et la transgression*. Paris: Bordas.

Eco, Umberto (1980). *The Name of the Rose*. London: Secker and Warburg, 1983.

Eliot, T. S. (1944). *Four Quartets*. London: Faber & Faber.

Ferenczi, S. (1924). *Thalassa, a Theory of Genitality*. New York: Psychoanalytic Quarterly. Reprinted London: Karnac Books, 1989.

Ferrater Mora, J. (1941). *Diccionario de filosofia*. Buenos Aires: Sudamericana, 1965.

Firpo, A., Veyne, P., Guerreau-Jalabert, A., Ruiz Domenec, J., Sot, M., Marchello-Nizzia, C., Teneti, A., Rossiaud, J., Perenoud, A., & Martínez Gros, G. (1984). *Amor, familia y sexualidad*. Barcelona: Argot.

Flem, L. (1986). *Freud et ses patients*. Paris: Hachette.

Foucault, M. (1963). Preface to: A transgression. In: *L'interdit et la transgression*. Paris: Bordas, 1983.

Freud, S. (1894a). The neuro-psychoses of defence. *S.E. 3*.

Freud, S. (1895b [1894]). On the grounds for detaching a particular syndrome from neurasthenia under the description "anxiety neurosis". *S.E. 3*.

Freud, S. (1900a). *The Interpretation of Dreams*. *S.E. 4–5*.

Freud, S.(1905c). *Jokes and Their Relation to the Unconscious*. *S.E. 8*.

Freud, S. (1905d). *Three Essays on the Theory of Sexuality. S.E. 7.*
Freud, S. (1908c). On the sexual theories of children. *S.E. 7.*
Freud, S. (1908d). "Civilized" sexual morality and modern nervous illness. *S.E. 9.*
Freud, S. (1910h). A special type of choice of object made by men. *S.E. 11.*
Freud, S. (1910c). *Leonardo da Vinci and a Memory of his Childhood. S.E. 11.*
Freud, S. (1912–13). *Totem and Taboo. S.E. 13.*
Freud, S. (1913c). The theme of the three caskets. *S.E. 12.*
Freud, S. (1913i). The disposition to obsessional neurosis. *S.E. 12.*
Freud, S. (1914c). On narcissism: An introduction. *S.E. 14.*
Freud, S. (1915c). Instincts and their vicissitudes. *S.E. 14.*
Freud, S. (1916–17). *Introductory Lectures on Psycho-Analysis. S.E. 15–16.*
Freud, S. (1918a). The taboo of virginity. *S.E. 11.*
Freud, S. (1919h). The uncanny. *S.E. 17.*
Freud, S. (1919e). A child is being beaten. *S.E. 17.*
Freud, S. (1923e). The infantile genital organisation. *S.E. 19.*
Freud, S. (1924c). The economic problem of masochism. *S.E. 19.*
Freud, S. (1924d). The dissolution of the Oedipus complex. *S.E. 19.*
Freud, S. (1925j). Some psychical consequences of the anatomical distinction between the sexes. *S.E. 19.*
Freud, S. (1926d [1925]). *Inhibitions, Symptoms and Anxiety. S.E. 20.*
Freud, S. (1926e). *The Question of Lay Analysis. S.E. 20.*
Freud, S. (1927e). Fetishism. *S.E. 21.*
Freud, S. (1930a). *Civilization and its Discontents. S.E. 21.*
Freud, S. (1931b). Female sexuality. *S.E. 21.*
Freud, S. (1933a). *New Introductory Lectures on Psycho-Analysis. S.E. 22.*
Freud, S. (1937c). Analysis terminable and interminable. *S.E. 23.*
Freud, S. (1937d). Constructions in analysis. *S.E. 23.*
Freud, S. (1940a [1938]). *An Outline of Psycho-Analysis. S.E. 23.*
Freud, S. (1940c [1922]). Medusa's head. *S.E. 18.*
Freud, S. (1941f [1938]). Findings, ideas, problems. *S.E. 23.*
Freud, S. (1950 [1892–1899]). Extracts from the Fliess papers. *S.E. 1.*
Freud, S. (1950 [1895]). Project for a scientific psychology. *S.E. 1.*
Garma, A. (1949). The origin of clothes. *Psychoanalytic Quarterly, 18* (2).
Gauthier, X. (n.d.). Pourquoi sorcières? *Sorcières, 24.*
Goldstein, R. (1983). El continente negro y sus enigmas. *Revista de Psicoanálisis, 7* (2).
Gori, R. (n.d.). Les murailles sonores. *L'Evolution Psychiatrique, 4*: 779–803.

Green, A. (1970). *L'Affect*. Paris: PUF.

Green, A. (1986). Pulsion de mort, narcissisme négatif, fonction des-objectalisante. In: *La pulsion de mort*. Paris: PUF.

Grimal, P. (1965). *Diccionario de la mitologia*. Barcelona: Labor.

Grunberger, B. (1973). Jalones para el estudio del narcisismo en la sexualidad femenina. In: *La sexualidad femenina, Nuevas apportaciones*. Barcelona: Laia.

Harris, M. (1974). *Vacas, cerdos, guerras y brujas*. Madrid: Alianza Editorial, 1986.

Hermann, I. (1930). *L'instinct filial*. Paris: Denoel, 1973.

Hite, S. (1987). Report. *Time* (12 October).

Horney, K. (1933). The denial of the vagina. In: *Feminine Psychology*. New York: W. W. Norton, 1967.

Hourcade, J. (1989). *L'Eglise est-elle mysogine?* Paris: Bibliothèque Centrale Pompidou.

Huston, N. (n.d.). Les vierges en lutte: de la rénovation d'un mythe. *Sorcières, 24*.

Institor, H. (Krämer, H.), & Sprenger, J. (1486). *Malleus Maleficarum*.

Jones, E. (1927). The early development of female sexuality. In: *Papers on Psycho-Analysis* (5th edition). London: Hogarth Press, 1948 [reprinted London: Karnac Books, 1977].

Jones, E. (1933). The phallic phase. In: *Papers on Psycho-Analysis* (5th edition). London: Hogarth Press, 1948 [reprinted London: Karnac Books, 1977].

Kaës, R., Missenard, A., Kaspi, R., Anzieu, D., Guillaumin, J., & Bleger, J. (1979). *Crise, rupture et depassement*. Paris: Dunod.

Kawabata, Y. (1969). *The House of the Sleeping Beauties*. Tokyo: Kodanska International.

Klein, M. (1964). *The Psycho-Analysis of Children*. London: Hogarth Press, 1975 [reprinted London: Karnac Books, 1998].

Kohut, H. (1965). Forms and transformations of narcissism. (Lecture given at the North American Psychoanalytical Association, New York, 5 December 1865.) *Journal of American Psychoanalytical Association, 14*, 1966.

Kohut, H. (1971). *The Analysis of the Self. The Psychoanalytic Study of the Child*, Monograph 4. New York: International Universities Press.

Kristeva, J. (1987). *Tales of Love*. New York: Columbia University Press.

Lacan, J. (1958). La signification du phallus. In: *Ecrit*. Paris: Seuil. *Ecrit: A Selection*. London: Tavistock, 1977.

Lacan, J. (1959–1960). *L'etique de la psychanalyse*. Paris: Seuil, 1986, Book VII. *The Ethics of Psychoanalysis*, New York: W. W. Norton, 1992.

Lacan, J. (1972–1973). *Encore*. Paris: Seuil, 1975.

Lacan, J. (1974). La tercera. In: *Acts of the Freudian School of Paris*. Barcelona: Petrel, 1980.

Langer, M. (1949). Viaje al centro de la tierra. Una fantasia de adolescente. *Revista de Psicoanálisis, 7* (1).

Langer, M. (1951). *Motherhood and Sexuality*. London: Free Association Books, 1991.

Laplanche, J., & Pontalis, J.-B. (1968). *The Language of Psychoanalysis*. London: Hogarth Press, 1973 [reprinted London: Karnac Books, 1996].

Laporte, R. (1975). Au delà de l'horreur vacui in Figures du vide. *Nouvelle Revue de Psychanalyse, 11* (Spring), 118.

Lawrence, D. H. (1933). The escaped cock [later retitled: The man who died]. In *Love among the Haystacks and other Stories*. Harmondsworth: Penguin Books, 1982.

Leclaire, S. (1979). Entrevista a la revista Imago. *Imago, 8*. Buenos Aires: Letra Viva.

Luquet-Parat, C. (1973). El cambio de objeto. In: *La sexualidad femenina*. Barcelona: Laia.

Marmor, J. (1952). Some considerations concerning orgasm in the female. In: Manfred de Martino, *Sexual Behaviour and Personality Characteristics*. New York: Citadel, 1963.

McDougall, J. (1986). *Corps et histoire*. Paris: Société d'édition "les belles lettres", 1986.

McDougall, J. (1989). *Theatres of the Body*. London: Free Association Books.

Mead, M. (1946). *Male and Female*. Harmondsworth: Penguin, 1970.

Mehler, S. (1988). Cien años después. In: A. M. Alizade (Ed.), *Voces de femineidad*. Buenos Aires: A. M. Alizade, 1991.

Merleau-Ponty, M. (1945). *Phenomenology of Perception*. London: Routledge, 1962.

Michelet, J. (1859). *La femme*. Paris: Flammarion, 1981.

Michelet, J. (1862). *La sorcière* (*La bruja*). Madrid: Akal, 1987.

Mom, J. (1956). Algunas consideraciones sobre el concepto de distancia en las fobias. *Revista de Psicoanálisis, 13* (4).

Monestier, M. (1963). *Les sociétés secrètes féminines*. Paris: Les Productions de Paris.

Moreau, T. (1991). La mégère apprivoisée. In: *La fidélité* (Series Morales, no. l). Paris: Editions Autrement.

Nasio, J. D. (1989). 7 *Conceptos fundamentales del psicoanálisis*. Barcelona: Gedisa.

Nobecourt-Granier, S. (1981). Freud et la virginité. In: *La première fois ou le roman de la virginité perdue à travers les siècles et les continents.* Paris: Ramsay.

Panoff, M. (1984). La sensualidad de los otros o el jardin del vecino. *Revista de Psicoanálisis, 42* (2), 1985.

Pérard, D. (1983). Rire en majeur. In: *L'interdit et la transgression.* Paris: Bordas.

Perez-Rioja, J.A. (1984). *Diccionario de simbolos y mitos.* Madrid: Tecnos.

Pernoud, R. (1980). *La mujer en el tempo de las catedrales.* Buenos Aires: Granica, 1987.

Perrot, P. (1984). *Le corps féminin.* Paris: Seuil.

Peyrefitte, A. (1977). *Le mythe de Penelope.* Paris: Gallimard.

Pommier, G. (1986). *La exception femenina.* Buenos Aires/Madrid: Alianza Estudio.

Rascovsky, A. (1973). Filicide. In: S. C. Feinstein (Ed.), *Adolescent Psychiatry,* Vol. 3. Chicago, IL: University of Chicago Press, 1974.

Rascovsky, A., & Rascovsky, M. (1977). Introducción al estudio psicoanalítico del psiquismo fetal. In: *El psiquismo fetal.* Buenos Aires: Paidòs.

Resnik, S. (1990). La madre arcaica y la funcion del padre. *Revista de Psicoanálisis, 67* (2).

Riviere, J. (1927). Womanliness as a masquerade. *International Journal of Psycho-Analysis, 10,* 303–313. [Also in: A. Hughes, *The Inner World and Joan Riviere.* London: Karnac Books, 1991.]

Rodrigué, E. (1987). *Ondina, Supertramp.* Buenos Aires: Sudamericana.

Rosolato, G. (1985). *Eléments de l'interpretation.* Paris: Gallimard.

Schust-Briat, G. (1991). "Gestes qui parlent, paroles qui cachent ou l'ecoute de l'indicible et les mots de l'innommable." Presented to the Congress of the European Federation of Psychoanalysis, Stockholm; Psychoanalysis in Europe, Bulletin 37, 22 March.

Sciarreta, R. (1986). Seminar given in a course on "The Four Basic Concepts of Lacan". Unpublished.

Sibony, D. (1991). Partage des eaux. In: *La fidelité* (Séries Morales, no.1). Paris: Editions Autrement.

Spitz, R. A. (1965). *The First Year of Life.* New York: International Universities Press, 1966.

Stern, D. N. (1985). *The Interpersonal World of the Infant.* London: Basic Books, 1986.

Thom, R. (1980). *Paraboles et catastrophes.* Paris: Champs Flammarion, 1983.

Urtubey, L. (1983). *Freud et le Diable.* Paris: PUF.

Vilaine-Montefiore, A. (n.d.). De qui suis-je en deuil? *Sorcières, 18.*

Vincent, J. (1986). *Biologie des Passions.* Paris: Odile Jacob.

Winnicott, D. W. (1953). Transitional objects and transitional phenomena. In: *Through Paediatrics to Psycho-Analysis.* London: Tavistock, 1958 [reprinted London: Karnac Books, 1992].

Winnicott, D. W. (1958). The capacity to be alone. In: *The Maturational Processes and the Facilitating Environment.* London: Hogarth Press, 1965 [reprinted London: Karnac Books, 1990].

Winnicott, D. W. (1966). The elements found in men and women. In: *Playing and Reality.* London: Routledge, 1971.

Yates, S. (1936). An investigation of the psychological factors in virginity and sexual defloration. *International Journal of Psycho-Analysis,* 2.

INDEX

Abadi, M., 165
abortion, 7
affect(s), body of, 34–50
affective memory, 34
Alizade, A. M., xii, 19, 51, 72, 133, 142, 166, 167, 168
Altamirano, N., 26
amphimixis of eroticism [Ferenczi], 88, 101
anaesthesia, sexual, 64, 66–67, 71, 84, 101, 104
Andreas-Salomé, L., 6, 87
annihilation, 38, 87, 94, 108, 170
  and masochism, 167–168
Anzieu, A., 18, 58, 100, 106
Anzieu, D., xiii, 2, 5–6, 10–12, 16–17, 29, 39–41, 43, 45, 51–52, 73, 75–77, 116, 137
Assoun, P. L., 7, 67, 118, 157
Aulagnier, P., 12, 18, 51, 55, 80, 128, 144, 151, 152, 153
Azzeo, R., 58

Bali, 82
Bataille, G., 56, 92–96, 108–109, 153, 155, 159, 168–169
Beam, L., 110
Bérouti, R., 109–110
Bick, E., 19, 116
birth trauma, 18
bisexuality, xiii, 4, 8, 61, 90–92, 133, 136–137, 146, 157
  woman's [Freud], 100
Bleger, J., 33
Blum, H., xii
Bodni, O., 59
body (*passim*):
  -to-body, 12, 37–39, 51–54, 75, 80, 155
  sense of, 9–23
Bonaparte, M., 84–85, 166, 169
Bowlby, J., 11, 40–41, 52

Cachard, C., 19
castration, 19, 83, 91, 98, 104, 107, 120, 129, 131, 133, 137
  anxiety, 57, 91
    and passion, 156
  phantasies of, 77, 145, 170
    and faithfulness, 143, 145
  and seduction, 42–50, 76
catastrophe, concept of [Thom], 28
Chambon, J., 108
Chasseguet-Smirgel, J., xii, 104, 133, 165
childbirth, 7, 63, 165–166, 168
Chrysostom, St John, 119
circularity, 20
clinical examples:
  Diana, 29–34
  Eva, 122–124
  Ines, 147–148
  Isabel, 158–159
  Maria, 91
  Mary, 20, 37, 39–50
  Mercedes, 165
  Mrs G [Anzieu], 106
  Mrs PJ [Freud], 69–70
  Nadine, 141, 148–149
  Sara, 118–119
  Teresa, 21–23
  Virginia, 125
container:
  –contained, differentiation between, 106
  psychic, 12, 16
    psychic envelope as, 29, 31
    skin-ego as, 40
continuity, 21
contrectation, instinct of [*Kontrektationstrieb*—Moll], 10, 52
Cosnier, J., 165, 166
Cournut, J., 92, 151, 152, 155

death, 6–7, 47, 55–57, 91, 93, 95, 99, 108–109, 120, 153, 160, 167–169
  castration-, 156
  and eroticism, feminine masochism as link between, 169
  instinct, xiii, 10, 28–29, 55, 75–76, 99, 103, 106, 108, 110
    vs. life-instinct, 10
  orgasm as, 108, 119
  -wishes, 20, 41, 104, 148
de Beauvoir, Simone, 125
demarcation signifiers [Rosolato], 11
depersonalization, 38, 55, 94, 99, 101
  and masochism, 166
Desroches-Noblecourt, C., 4
Dickinson, R. L., 110
discontinuity, 21
Dolto, F., 52, 83, 85
Dorey, R., 93, 94, 95

Eco, U., 113
ego-libido, vs. object-libido [Freud], 10
Eliade, M., 26
Eliot, T. S., 117
Eluard, P., 139
emerging self, infant's, sense of [Stern], 26
Enriquez, M., 19, 41
envelope(s), 20–21
  functions of, 29
  narcissistic, 26, 29
  psychic, 54
    and circularity, 20
    [clinical example: Teresa], 21–23
    and nucleus of stone, 29–34
"erection", feminine [Freud], 67–68
Eros, 20, 39, 42, 53, 115, 166
eroticism, 163–170
  of bodies, 56, 109
  diffusion of, 62, 80, 86, 100, 130
  of hearts, 56, 109
  oral, 81

sacred, 56, 109, 159, 167
sublimated, 57
Esquirol, J. E., 146
Etchegoyen, R. H., xi–xiv
"experiential mass", body as, 9, 17, 34

faithfulness:
archaic, 141
forms of, 141
to primal object, 80
femininity, primordial, 128
Ferenczi, S., 86, 88, 89, 101, 108, 167
fidelity/infidelity, 8, 139–149
Firpo, A., 1
Flem, L., 85
Fliess, W., 67, 70, 157
fluidification and secretion, 3
formal signifiers [Anzieu], 11, 12
Foucault, M., 92, 93, 96
Freud, S., xi–xiv, 2, 4, 7, 19, 20, 25–26, 52, 54, 62, 72, 76, 78, 81–87, 93, 101, 104, 106, 109–110, 120, 122, 124–125, 127–129, 131, 132, 142, 152
on affects, 35, 36, 38, 39
on breast-feeding orgasm, xiii
on erogenicity, 3
on faithfulness/unfaithfulness, 144
on feminine bisexuality, 100
on feminine masochism, 163–164, 168, 170
on feminine regression, 89–90
on feminine sexuality, 64–71, 84
on instincts, categories of, 10
on men's fear of femininity, 91
on Mother-Nature, 94
on myth of Moerae, 169
on Oedipus complex in girls, 128, 130
on perception, 13–14
on phallic mother, 82–83
phallocentric theory of, xi
on pleasure, 99
on regression, 90, 105
on repression, 86
schema of sexuality of, 74
self-analysis of, 157
on "a sort of regression", 85–90
theory of sexual monism of, xi
on virginity, 114
frigidity, 3, 69, 71, 92, 98, 101, 105, 120, 130, 144

Garma, A., 18, 136
Gauguin, E. H. P., 7
Gauthier, X., 132
Goldstein, R., 84
Greece, 12
Green, A., 35, 38, 103
Grunberger, B., 133

Harris, M., 159
hate, radical, 55
helplessness, 36, 38
state of [*Hilflosigkeit*], 154
[Rosenberg], 166
primordial, 30, 128, 154
Hera, 62
Hermann, I., 11
Hippocrates, 119
Hite, S., 105
holding, 16
homosexuality, in ancient Greece, 12
Horney, K., 62
Hourcade, J., 114
Huston, N., 119
hysteria, 58, 67, 100, 101
archaic concept of, 12

idealization, and faithfulness, 143
incest, 77, 80, 88, 119
taboo, 5, 76
instinct(s), 9–13, 26, 52–53, 76, 99, 105, 110, 160, 164
and affects, 34
of apprehension [Hermann], 11
of attachment [Bowlby], 11, 52

instinct(s) (*continued*):
categories of [Freud], 10
concept of, 10–11
of contrectation [*Kontrektationstrieb*—Moll], 10, 52, 122
death: *see* death, instinct
of destruction, 6, 17, 169
to dominate, 10, 53, 76, 143
male, 167
to enwrap oneself, 29
of knowledge, 122, 160
life, 6, 10, 17, 29, 75, 99
partial, 99
and passion, 152
of pleasure, 99
of self-preservation [Freud], 10, 37, 52, 72, 73, 76, 77, 154
sex, 10, 73, 76, 77, 122
feminine, 64
narcissistic, 37
taming of, 116, 152, 157

Jones, E., xii, 62, 81, 87
Joyce, J., 54

Kawabata, Y., 57
Klein, M., 62, 81, 87, 100, 105, 110, 120
Kristeva, J., 117, 119

Lacan, J., 35, 51, 53, 100, 102, 107, 129, 133, 167
lactation, 63, 81
primal orgasm during, 72
Laporte, R., 131
Lawrence, D. H., 118
Leclaire, S., 4
Leonardo da Vinci [Freud], 78, 81
libidinal development, stages of, xi
life instinct, 6, 10, 17, 29, 57, 75, 99
linearity, 20
masculine, 64
"lines of loss" and faithfulness, 144
love, true [*echte Liebe*—Freud], 53, 142

Luquet-Parat, C., 45, 87

Marmor, J., 110
masochism, 17, 29, 43
biological, 164
erogenous, 104, 164, 165
primal, 166
feminine, 8, 163–170
clinical point of view, 163–167
philosophical point of view, 168–170
moral, 147, 164, 165
sado-, 143
McDougall, J., 12, 37, 88
Mead, M., 5, 82
menstruation, 7, 63, 87, 124
Merleau-Ponty, M., 14, 15, 16, 52, 102
Michelet, J., 145, 146, 158
Moll, A., 10, 52
Monestier, M., 12, 114
Moreau, T., 145, 146
mother–child dyad, 129
and faithfulness, 140
and first primordial orgasm, 51
intimacy of, 115
pathological asymmetry in, 154
mourning, 38, 57, 59, 118, 147, 148
for loss of libido [Freud], 66

narcissism, 52, 54, 57–59, 100–104, 115, 130–133, 137, 148, 168
feminine, 104, 144
infantile, 19, 83
and passion, 154
primary, xiii, 73
Nasio, J. D., 130
Neruda, P., 25, 26
Nobecourt-Granier, S., 117
Nora, 134–137
nuclear self, infant's, sense of [Stern], 26

object-libido vs. ego-libido [Freud], 10

objet à [Lacan], 100
Oedipus complex, 83, 137, 140, 141, 147
  in women, dissolution [*Untergang*] of, 127–137
orgasm(s):
  feminine, 3, 61–111
    and men, 90–92
  infinite [Cournut], 92
  primal, 71–75, 80, 103
  "sort of", infantile [Freud], xiii, 71–75, 128

Panoff, M., 145
Parent-Auber, 145
parricide, 76, 80
parthenogenesis, 115
  symmetry of, 153
passion, 151–161
  amorous, 153–154
  asymmetry of, 153
  in corporal space, 155
  in extracorporeal space, 155
  objects of, 152, 156
  in temporal space, 155
  types of [Aulagnier], 151
penis:
  envy, 61, 63, 97–98, 104, 129–130, 132–133, 147
  role of for male, 61
  universality of, 7
Pérard, D., 93
perception, 13–16
Perrot, P., 4
perversion, 164
  masochistic, 164
  sexual, 81, 101
Peyrefitte, A., 142
phallocentric theory [Freud], xi
pleasure principle, xiii, 73
"pollution" [Freud], 68, 70, 110
pregnancy, 20, 63, 136
primal language, 16
primal object, 19
primary narcissism, xiii
primordial orgasm, xiii, 51

Radó, S., xiii
Rank, O., 18
Rascovsky, A., 19, 20
Rascovsky, M., 20
regression, 12, 15, 55, 101, 106–108, 135
  feminine, 89
  and masochism, 166, 167
  "a sort of" [Freud], 85–90, 105
  thalassic [Ferenczi], 86, 89, 92, 100, 108
repression, transference as, 85–90
Resnik, S., 32
Riviere, J., 130
Rodrigué, E., 92
Rosolato, G., 11

saint and witch, 159–161
Samoa, 5
Schust-Briat, G., 11
Sciarreta, R., 35, 99
sensation, 13–16
sensoriality and erogenousness, 21–23
sensuality, affective, 38
senti, 5, 16, 20, 29, 39, 51, 76
separation anxiety and faithfulness, 143
sexuality:
  dualistic theory of, xii
  feminine, Freud's concept of, 64–71
  schema of [Freud], 64–71, 66, 74
sexual monism, theory of [Freud], xi
Sibony, D., 143, 144
skin:
  -ego, xiii, 2, 6, 16–19, 23, 29, 41, 52, 58, 73, 116, 141
    container function of, 40
    filtering, 40, 116
    space of, 16–17
  psychic, 20
Spitz, R. A., 5, 11, 16, 51
Stern, D. N., 26, 35, 88

stone, nucleus of, 25–59, 73
Strachey, J., 170
subjective self, infant's, sense of [Stern], 26
sublimation, 6, 10, 56–57, 78, 117, 122, 160, 161
  and orgasm of the ego [Winnicott], 111
  and transgression, 78, 94

Thanatos, 20, 39, 53, 166
Thom, R., 28
Tibet, 12
Tiresias, 62, 92
touch(ing), 2, 22, 38, 51, 73, 75–80, 88, 110, 121
  adult, 79–80
  prohibition, 76–79
  whole body, 75–76
transference, 38, 84, 85–90, 149
  erogenous, 23
  erotic, heterosexual, 33
transgression [Bataille], 92–96

unfaithfulness, 80, 139–149

verbal self, infant's, sense of [Stern], 26
Vilaine-Montefiore, A., 91
Vincent, J., 151, 154
virginities, feminine, 113–125

Winnicott, D. W., 10, 54, 111, 146
witch, 4, 92, 102
  and psychoanalysis, 156–159
  and saint, 159–161

Yañez, A., 158